HOW TO DO RESTORATIVE PEER MEDIATION IN YOUR SCHOOL

by the same author

A Practical Introduction to Restorative Practice in Schools
Theory, Skills and Guidance
Bill Hansberry
Foreword by Margaret Thorsborne
ISBN 978 1 84905 707 3
eISBN 978 1 78450 232 4

of related interest

What are you staring at?
A Comic About Restorative Justice in Schools
Pete Wallis and Joseph Wilkins
ISBN 978 1 78592 016 5
eISBN 978 1 78450 260 7

Restorative Practice and Special Needs
A Practical Guide to Working Restoratively with Young People
Nick Burnett and Margaret Thorsborne
Foreword by Nancy Riestenberg
ISBN 978 1 84905 543 7
eISBN 978 0 85700 968 5

The KidsKope Peer Mentoring Programme
A Therapeutic Approach to Help Children and Young People Build Resilience and Deal with Conflict
Nina Wroe and Penny McFarlane
ISBN 978 1 84905 500 0
eISBN 978 0 85700 903 6

Implementing Restorative Practice in Schools
A Practical Guide to Transforming School Communities
Margaret Thorsborne and Peta Blood
ISBN 978 1 84905 377 8
eISBN 978 0 85700 737 7

HOW TO DO RESTORATIVE PEER MEDIATION IN YOUR SCHOOL

A Quick Start Kit –
Including Online Resources

BILL HANSBERRY and
CHRISTIE-LEE HANSBERRY

Jessica Kingsley *Publishers*
London and Philadelphia

First published in 2018
by Jessica Kingsley Publishers
73 Collier Street
London N1 9BE, UK
and
400 Market Street, Suite 400
Philadelphia, PA 19106, USA

www.jkp.com

Library of Congress Cataloging in Publication Data
A CIP catalog record for this book is available from the Library of Congress

British Library Cataloguing in Publication Data
A CIP catalogue record for this book is available from the British Library

ISBN 978 1 78592 384 5
eISBN 978 1 78450 736 7

Printed and bound in Great Britain

Contents

1

INTRODUCTION
Restorative Peer Mediators in Your School

Peer mediation

The idea of skilling older students to help younger students is not a new one. Peer mediation has been around in many schools in varying forms for a long time as a vehicle to skill students in the processes of conflict resolution.

When done well, peer mediator programs increase a climate of care and cooperation in schoolyards. In some instances, peer mediation programs can free up teachers to address the more serious problems that arise while peer mediators assist peers with low-level social problems and conflicts. On this, we have to be clear – peer mediation programs should never be about passing adult duty of care over to students. Peer mediator programs, however, do call on senior students to take care of younger students by increasing the number of caring and watchful eyes in schoolyards and playgrounds.

What's in it for students?
Required helpfulness

It is very good for the wellbeing of young people to be asked to help others. Young people who learn that they can belong to their school through their contributions do better and feel more connected to their school. Wellbeing experts have known for some time that young people do better in environments that require them to contribute by helping others. Emmy Werner's famous research on resilience found that the most resilient children are required to carry out socially desirable tasks to prevent others in their community experiencing overload, distress or discomfort (Werner 1984). Such acts, which Werner called 'required helpfulness', have been proven to deliver lasting positive emotional changes in young people. In a similar vein, many cultures share common teachings that humans can reach heights of happiness, fulfilment and connection to others (that we all seek) when they commit to a way of living that maintains a focus on being helpful to others (offering service) without expectation of anything in return.

Restorative schools and an expectation of care

Restorative schools are places where all students are asked to take care of one another. Whether this means taking responsibility for misdeeds and making amends, taking part in a restorative circle to address issues that affect whole groups or being part of a caring circle to help a classmate form and maintain social connections, students in *restorative schools* are required to take an active interest in one another and to show care. Naturally, this extends to responsibilities that are unique to senior students in a school, and often peer mediation is one of these. This book will outline a model of restorative peer mediation (RPM), which is tailored for peer mediation in restorative schools.

Younger students feel safer when they see older students as caring people who have an interest in them. We can all remember looking up at older kids when we were just starting school. They looked like adults to us and had enormous potential to make us feel safe and supported, or to frighten us. This is the reason why buddy programs have flourished in schools in recent years.

Allowing boys to nurture

The idea of taking care of younger students is something that is often unconsciously associated with girls. Primary or elementary teaching, in particular, remains a female-dominated profession, despite efforts to encourage more males to teach this age group. This can perpetuate the myth that boys are excluded from nurturing roles; in other words, taking care of others is not something that boys do. This mindset needs to be challenged for the sake of our boys.

In middle and senior settings, it is equally, if not more important to be deliberate about implementing and maintaining programs that involve young males with each other in a pastoral sense. Ian Lillico (2000), in his Churchill Fellowship work on boys, made an important observation:

> When boys are given responsibility they grow. If, later, that responsibility is taken away again, we will face boys who disengage and become increasingly hostile and unmanageable. Schools must be particularly aware of this as boys progress annually through classes – that the degree of responsibility gradually increases from year to year. This should form a part of Whole School Planning. It is particularly important at the Primary School/Secondary School interface that the degree of responsibility students possess at the end of their Primary Schooling is tapped into and that students are not made to regress on entering their Secondary Schooling. This is the cause of many boys disengaging from school once entering High School and schools must take every step to stop what is happening around Australia. (Recommendation 15)

Adolescence is a tumultuous developmental stage where young people are pulled back and forth between the questions: 'How do I belong?', 'How do I *size up* compared to others' and 'What makes me stand out from the crowd (how am I unique)?' Belonging is a communal game. We humans *belong best* through our efforts toward common group goals and activities aimed at making someone else's life a bit easier. Feeling helpful (even needed) is what makes us happy. This is a message that must echo through all aspects of school life if we want to keep young people connected to their school. We truly believe that required helpfulness, in terms of efforts to improve the wellbeing of another, is an important protective factor in adolescence and prevents many young men from falling into the abyss of individualism and emotional isolation, which can be outcomes of narrow and limiting construction of masculinity (ideas about what it is to be a boy/man). We have to work hard to give boys *permission* to engage with one another in a pastoral, nurturing sense, not just a competitive sense.

It is vitally important that schools communicate to boys that nurturing isn't just something, we think, they can do, rather, it's something we *require* them to do. Working in a role such as RPM allows boys to broaden their ideas of *what it means to be a boy* and provides an outlet for what we believe to be part of boys' innate character. We have seen, over and over, the tremendous positive changes in adolescent boys' attitudes and engagement and behaviour at school when they have been asked to *step up* into a position of caring and mentoring. The RPM program is an ideal context for this to take place.

What's in it for an *aspiring* restorative school?

For schools that are in the implementation phase of restorative practices (the first three years or so), we see an RPM program as a *bottom-up* approach to spreading a restorative ethos through a school.

Imagine the momentum that is created by having staff and senior students working concurrently to develop the language and skills of restorative problem solving. How would students feel about the chance to learn something alongside their teachers (*with* teachers) instead if just having Restorative Practices as something that is done *to* them? How would staff respond to being on a learning journey with students? This is truly powerful stuff that we have seen supercharge the implementation of Restorative Practices in schools.

What's in it for an *established* restorative school?

For schools that have the full continuum of Restorative Practices working (typically, after two to three years), RPM becomes a very important program that helps to embed Restorative Practices as 'the way we do things around here'. When students and teachers share a common language around helping one another, Restorative Practices become more deeply embedded in the school's culture. Restorative Peer Mediators (RPMs) become a very powerful agent in the transmission of culture of understanding, peacefulness and reparation to younger students who are new to the school.

Which students make good RPMs?

It's understandable that when considering candidates for an RPM program that many schools immediately think of their *responsible kids* – their *role models*. Our experience from years of working in many schools is that enormous human potential goes untapped when only the usual *star students* are considered for RPM programs.

We've found that the best RPM groups contain the students who've *done it tough* at school and know what it is like to have been involved in conflict and strife. After all, it's fairly likely that it is these students who have had the most exposure to restorative processes! At a deeper level, however, for students who've been on the receiving end of restorative processes, a chance to use these processes to help others allows them to see themselves, and how they belong to the school, in a different way.

Young people who've *done it tough* bring incredible insights from their own experiences and often are more able to empathize with the tricky thoughts and feelings that others experience when involved in conflict or incidents of harm. We've seen *troubled* students reinvent themselves through involvement in programs that place them in positions of caring responsibility. It is often the case that young people only start to reflect on their own habitual responses to conflict when they become involved with others in a pastoral sense.

So, we urge you, to get the most of an RPM program, take a risk and go for a mixture of students. Approach young people who you wouldn't normally consider as your RPMs and encourage them to be part of the program. In the vast majority of cases, they won't let you down.

Creating and maintaining a case for RPMs in your school

Before leaping into selecting and training RPMs, we believe there are some important steps that will provide powerful evidence of the effectiveness and longevity of an RPM program.

We've all seen effective programs and initiatives go by the wayside because a new leader to the school fails to recognize the benefits to the school's culture. Many of us have kicked ourselves for not gathering data at the outset of a new program or initiative, so we have had nothing to show in terms of quantitative evidence when we've been asked to produce it. This is real life and we all need to be much smarter in how we prove the efficacy of any program that competes for limited resources such as staff time and budget dollars. This is where we need to collect some data before we start. You don't have to reinvent the wheel. We suggest you do some hypothesizing about what benefits a school that implements an RPM program might see:

- What might you expect to see in the number of yard incidents handled by duty staff when RPMs are trained and 'on duty'?

- What might you expect to hear from your teachers about what has changed in the yard when their work is supported by a trained group of RPMs?

- What might change in the way your younger students see older students and how safe they feel in their presence?

- What might change in regards to how safe younger students feel in the schoolyard?

- What might change in how students view different parts of the schoolyard when asked to rate them as places in which they feel safe or unsafe?

- How might an RPM program change how the young people involved feel about school and their place in the school?

- What might you expect to hear from their teachers about the general levels of engagement of RPMs?

When you do a little brainstorming about *what might change* after the implementation of the RPM program, many possibilities come to mind about what could be measured to prove its viability. A simple *pre- and post-design* that gets some measurable data (quantitative and qualitative) will build a powerful case for an RPM program and also give some very important information about changes that might need to be made to support the program.

We suggest that you sit down with your principal and look over the previous year's data on existing measures of *student wellbeing* and *student perceptions* of the schoolyard and look for a few data sets that you'd expect an RPM program to influence. This exercise will really get the juices flowing around great lines of enquiry on issues of yard safety and student wellbeing.

After 12 months of an RPM program, simply compare data sets. Has there been some change? Can part of this be attributed to the inclusion of the RPMs? We know that you'll be pleasantly surprised with the results.

Links to curricula

At the end of this guide is an appendix which lays out the links to curricula around the world (Appendix 7).

The RPM selection process

After an RPM program has been running in a school for a year or more, you will hear students talk with enthusiasm about hopefully becoming an RPM. There will be a *buzz* around the prospect of getting into the program. Creating this culture is an important part of the process.

Selecting the RPM cohort

In a primary (elementary) schools, the senior students take on the responsibility of becoming RPMs.

In secondary school settings this isn't as simple. There will be students entering secondary school who will have already been involved as RPMs as the seniors in their last school. To suddenly deny them any opportunity to continue this work would be an awful waste, not to mention the message this would send to them about their loss of seniority in their new school. These students can still be put to work providing RPM services to same age peers (if they are the youngest cohort in the school).

Selling the RPM program to students

Successful RPM schools work at communicating to students that being an RPM is a *big deal*, making it a respected and sought after role of responsibility within the school. To do this, it is important to *sell* the program to the group of students that you will be inviting to apply. Present a clear picture of the attributes, skills and qualities required by students in order to be effective RPMs. This may be shared in a presentation to the year level from which you are asking for applications. Be sure to stress to students:

- The importance of RPMs to the school

  » RPMs play an important role with teachers in making the yard kind, fair and safe

  » RPMs help to teach restorative thinking and behaviour to students

- The opportunity to lead and support other students

  » In primary settings, RPMs show young students that older students in the school are friendly and kind

  » In primary settings, RPMs help show younger students how to solve tricky situations and friendship problems

  » In secondary settings, RPMs are students who are specially trained to help de-escalate conflict and work with peers to resolve issues. These may be the same age or older than the students they are helping

- The obligations and expectations

  » RPMs will be donating up to one break time a week to be on duty

  » RPMs will be expected to attend meetings and phase 2 training sessions

- The rewards of the position

  » RPMs are looked up to by younger students in the school

» RPMs are seen by students as having specialized skills in conflict resolution and an interest in helping others

» RPMs see themselves as being an important part of the school's wellbeing/pastoral care processes.

Getting students to talk at home about being an RPM

Following the information-sharing session(s), encourage interested students to talk with their parents about becoming an RPM. This is important for both primary- and secondary-aged students. Many young people live very full lives – involvement in sports teams, special interest groups and other extracurricular endeavours. Talking with parents at home can help students think about whether they can manage the commitment involved with being an RPM. Talking with parents about the RPM program may also prompt important conversations about service to others, volunteering and community leadership.

It's a good idea to put an article in the school newsletter or send a note/message home to students in that year level. It's important that parents understand the significance of *required helpfulness* to the wellbeing of young people and how being an RPM requires students to make a sacrifice of time for the wellbeing of others.

The application

Interested students are given an RPM Job and Person Specification (see the example on page 15). They then create an application addressing the qualities on the Job and Person Specification.

Making RPM a unit within a subject

The strong links to many existing national curriculm documents (see Appendix 7) make involvement in the RPM program suitable for whole classes to engage in as part of their curriculum in both primary and secondary settings.

The training day can be easily broken up and used as the basis for a unit of work on relationships and conflict. Of course, not all students would be interested in extending this into actual RPM work, but particular students with a keen interest could go on to become part of the RPM team. In effect, the school's normal curriculum would become a recruitment tool for the RPM program.

The supplementary materials and all worksheets marked with ∗ are available to download and print from www.jkp.com/catalogue/book/9781785923845

RPM Job and Person Specification

(Early Years & Primary)

Role description

Restorative Peer Mediators (RPMs) have an important role in working with school staff to support younger students at play times when upsets arise. RPMs work with students to help fix problems and upsets by asking restorative questions that focus on the issue and help students to find their own solutions to a problem. RPMs do not *tell students* what *to do* or give advice; they support younger students to find their own solutions. This is an important part of building problem solving skills and resilience in our younger students.

Qualities we look for in an RPM

> » Kind and caring to others

> » Fair and understanding – doesn't take sides

> » A good listener – lets others talk

> » Can stay calm in tricky moments

> » Can be trusted

> » Reliable – shows up when they are needed

> » Confident and friendly around younger students

The commitment we need from an RPM

You will need to be committed to both phases of the RPM training program in order to develop the skills you need to be an RPM. You will also be required to give up one playtime per week as well as some lesson time each fortnight for phase 2 trainings. This might involve you catching up with classwork that is missed.

To apply: Tell us how you would make a good RPM?

Please write an exposition (or create an audio, video clip or another form of presentation), giving examples of ways and times you have used the qualities above to help others (at school and out of school) and how you will show them as an RPM.

Please send applications to:

Applications close:

RPM Job and Person Specification

(Middle & Secondary)

Role description

Restorative Peer Mediators (RPMs) have an important role in working with school staff to support peers through moments of conflict. RPMs work with other students to help resolve problems and upsets by asking restorative questions that focus on the issue and help students to find their own solutions to a problem. RPMs do not *tell students what to do* or give advice; they support other students to find their own solutions. This is an important part of building problem solving skills and resilience.

Qualities we look for in an RPM

» Kind and caring to others

» Fair and understanding – doesn't take sides

» A good listener – lets others talk

» Can stay calm in tricky moments

» Can be trusted

» Reliable – shows up when they are needed

» Confident and friendly around younger students

The commitment we need from an RPM

You will need to be committed to both phases of the RPM training program in order to develop the skills you need to be an RPM. You will also be required to give up one break time per week as well as some lesson time each fortnight for phase 2 trainings. This will involve you negotiating with subject teachers about catching up with classwork that is missed or requesting extensions on assignments. Being an RPM doesn't guarantee that you will be granted extensions on assignments.

To apply: Tell us how you would make a good RPM?

Please write an exposition (or create an audio, video clip or another form of presentation), giving examples of ways and times you have used the qualities above to help others (at school and out of school) and how you will show them as an RPM.

Please send applications to:

Applications close:

Alternatives to written applications

Because writing is a barrier to some students with specific learning difficulties such as dyslexia, encourage applications in forms other than just written. Students may wish to submit a PowerPoint presentation or an audio or video clip of them addressing the application criteria or to present to you personally. The amount of effort that students put into these alternative modes of application often gives wonderful insight into a student's dedication to becoming an RPM.

When applications are submitted

RPMs are selected from the pool of applicants by the RPM program coordinator and relevant school staff. A good number of RPMs to choose is 15–20 students. Of course, this will vary depending on the size of your school.

As mentioned earlier, RPMs may not end up being your *model students* (in the traditional sense of the term). What matters most is how the applicants interact with and treat other, younger students. A balanced group of RPMs will include a cross-section of students to ensure that different ethnicities, genders, socioeconomic levels and academic abilities are represented.

Keeping parents in the loop

Parent cooperation is important for the success of the program, particularly in the primary years. In the middle and secondary years, because involvement in the RPM program may impede on some lesson time, it is important that parents are aware of their child's involvement so that they can discuss the time management implications with their child.

After the RPMs have been selected, a letter informing parents of their child's selection as an RPM, their responsibilities and a permission form will need to be signed by each child's parent or guardian. Below is an example letter that places the RPM program within the broader context of the school's restorative philosophy and wellbeing policies.

Dear Parents/Caregivers,

Our School is proud to announce that your son/daughter has been successful with their application to become a Restorative Peer Mediator (RPM).

Our school is a conflict positive school. This means that we understand that conflicts, although distressing, are an inevitable part of school life and need to be dealt with head-on and not swept under the carpet. Our staff are trained in restorative conflict resolution strategies and we believe that it is important that our students are as well.

At times, students become involved in problems and conflicts during break times and sometimes these conflicts can be worked out with the help of students trained as Restorative Peer Mediators (RPMs). RPMs are specially trained students who help other students sort out conflicts. The RPMs are trained to listen well, be neutral and not to take sides. Our RPMs use *restorative processes* to help students listen to one another, understand the problem from the other's perspective and solve problems. These are the very skills all young people need to be able to work well with others, not just at school, but in workplaces, too.

The RPM program sits within our school policies in regards to Restorative Practices to teach students resilient problem solving qualities. Your son/daughter has generously committed to helping other students in this way and we are very grateful to them and to all the students who applied to be an RPM.

RPMs will be involved in a full day (phase 1) training prior to becoming a mediator. They will then be involved in the more important fortnightly (phase 2) training sessions during their tenure as an RPM. Please feel free to talk with your child about these ongoing responsibilities as trainings and meetings will sometimes clash with other important parts of school life. There may be times when RPMs will be asked to catch up with class work they missed while doing RPM duties.

This will be a great experience for your son/daughter.

Sincerely,

Coordinator: Restorative Peer Mediation

✂ --

I give _____ (child's name) permission to participate in the Restorative Peer Mediation program and training day on _____. This training will be held at school in _____. I also consent to my child being involved in the ongoing RPM work, including further phase 2 training meetings.

Parent signature _____

Date _____

*Please sign and return this tear-off slip as soon as possible.

★

Phase 1 training

The whole-day phase 1 training aims to train the new RPMs in the basics of Restorative Practices and how to facilitate low-level conferences (restorative chats) between students to help them with conflicts and upsets in the yard.

This training works best when in a place away from the normal classroom setting, possibly off-site or in a room free from distractions. Think of the phase 1 training day like an in-service you would go to yourself. Provide morning tea and refreshments. This all adds to the *kudos* of the program and shows your respect for the students who have volunteered their time for the school and the important RPM work ahead.

Outcomes of the RPM training day – an overview

- RPMs can define what Restorative Peer Mediation is.

- RPMs consider different causes of conflict at their school.

- RPMs identify the types of issues they can help with and types of issues they will refer to a staff member.

- RPMs learn about listening and questioning for understanding.

- RPMs learn how to use a specially modified Restorative Conference Script.

- RPMs practice using the script through role-play scenarios.

- RPMs take part in discussion and decision-making for implementing the Peer Mediation program in the school.

Informing the community about the RPM program

Use any methods at your disposal to inform the school community about the RPM program – newsletters, text messages, school website and social media.

Because nothing beats a personal touch, after the phase 1 training, arrange for primary-aged RPMs to visit classrooms to introduce themselves and talk with younger students about their job in the schoolyard. It's important for young students to be able to see and hear the RPMs. In a secondary setting, get the new RPMs to introduce themselves at Year Level and whole school assemblies or during pastoral care group times.

An example script of what the RPMs might say in these introductory classroom visits follows.

Suggested script to use when RPMs introduce themselves to classes

(Primary)

Hi. My name is _____ and this is _____.

You might remember us. We are two of the new Restorative Peer Mediators here at school. We call ourselves RPMs for short. You can, too, if you like!

We are here to remind you that if you are having a problem in the yard that you can't sort out on your own, you can come and talk to one of us, or any other RPM you see in the yard. We will be wearing a bright vest like the ones we are wearing now. We will be near the playground and will have our clipboards, our badges and jackets on so that you can see us easily.

It's really important that you know about some rules that everyone must follow when they come to an RPM to sort out a problem. We call these the *RPM Rules of Engagement*:

» Listen to each other

» Speak one at a time

» Tell the truth

» Try hard to solve the problem.

If you can't do this, we will not be able to help you and might send you to a teacher on duty.

So, if you are outside playing and you have a problem with someone who you would like some help sorting out, look out for us or another Restorative Peer Mediator.

What questions do people have?

Suggested script to use when RPMs introduce themselves to classes

(Middle & Secondary)

Hi. Our names are _____.

We are part of the Restorative Peer Mediators Program. We call ourselves RPMs for short.

Our job is to help people who find themselves in a conflict with other students. Getting caught in a conflict, particularly if it gets loud, can be really embarrassing and sometimes you feel like the only option you have is to fight, abuse others or trash them on social media. This always gets ugly and usually has no clear winner! This is where we might be able to help.

If you are having a problem in the yard that you can't sort out, we are trained to help. It's not our job to break up fights or situations where people have lost their minds and things have gotten dangerous, we want to help before things get to that point.

As uncool as it may look, you will be able to spot us in the yard. We'll be the ones in the vests/badges. Please don't makes jokes of us, we don't think we are any better than anyone else, we just want to help people if they are in conflict and don't see a way out.

If you do want our help, there are some rules that everyone must follow:

> » Listen to each other

> » Speak one at a time

> » Tell the truth

> » Try hard to solve the problem.

If you can't do this, we will not be able to help you. It's as simple as that!

Thanks for your time. Any questions?

Other RPM essentials

Duty roster

After the phase I training day, create a duty roster for the RPMs. Ideally, every RPM will have an opportunity to be on duty once a week. This will give them the necessary practice they need to hone the skills they've learned during the phase I training day. It's important to have RPMs *on the beat* as soon after their phase I training as possible.

Training too many RPMs for the program can limit the *on the job* time for RPMs. Training too few RPMs will obviously require RPMs to give up more than one session a week. Nobody wants burnt-out RPMs!

You might consider even having most, if not all of your RPMs rostered on in the week following the phase I training to give them the best chance to practice the skills while they are fresh in their mind. Of course, this will mean there will be a lot of RPMs on duty at one time, but no harm can come from this!

Visibility of RPMs in the schoolyard

It is important for students to be able to find the RPMs in the yard. In primary settings, it can help to designate a series of places where RPMs can be found. If your yard behaviour data indicates particular *hot spots* in the yard where more conflicts occur, or where many students have reported feeling unsafe, you might consider making these the designated RPM areas. In middle and secondary settings, RPMs might be identifiable by a badge only. Adolescents are often sensitive about standing out too much, so a brightly coloured vest may be overkill. Discuss this with the RPMs to gauge their level of comfort with how they will be made visible.

In some schools, a challenge we've experienced is RPMs reporting that there hasn't been much to do during their duty period and so they've expressed that they could be with their friends instead of being *stuck on duty* and doing nothing. Enthusiasm for the role naturally wains (understandably) when this happens. In this case, an alternative is to create an arrangement where RPMs can go about their normal yard activities at break times, but wear an RPM high-visibility vest so they are easily visible. The understanding being that if needed, they will stop what they are doing and fulfil their RPM duties. If this option is used, it needs to by widely understood that an RPM can be approached, no matter what they are doing because they are *on call*. How this happens will depend on the geographical layout of your school grounds, as RPMs still need to be accessible.

We strongly recommend investing in professionally produced badges for RPMs (similar to staff badges). These cost very little and they speak volumes to your RPMs, and other students, about how much the RPMs are valued within the school. High-visibility vests are also recommended for RPMs. With secondary students, too much visibility may be plain uncool, so there is a balance to be struck between not making RPMs too conspicuous while ensuring they are still identifiable as RPMs. Consult with the RPMs on this matter as making these types of decisions without them may lead to the program's demise!

The RPM folder

When on duty, RPMs need to carry their folders, which they are given and explained about during phase 1 training (see page 31). These folders should contain the *RPM Rules* on the front cover. On the inside of the folder is the modified Restorative Script as well as recording sheets where the RPMs record the *more serious* issues they have been involved with, as well as any issues that may need follow-up from either teachers or RPMs during the next break time.

The RPM program implementation process in a nutshell

1. Students are introduced to the role and responsibilities of RPMs and are invited to apply to be an RPM.

2. Applications are looked at by staff and a group of students are selected to be a part of the peer mediation program by the RPM coordinator in collaboration with relevant staff.

3. Parents are informed of their child's participation in the program via a letter with a return permission slip.

4. The RPM group participates in *phase 1 training* – a whole-day training session planned and facilitated by the RPM coordinator.

5. The RPM program is promoted to the school community through assembly announcements, a newsletter, school-based social media and any other appropriate form of communication.

6. RPMs visit classrooms to introduce themselves and talk to each class about their role.

7. RPMs plan and give a short presentation at Whole School Assembly/during pastoral care sessions that dramatizes (primary settings) or communicates (middle & secondary) what a peer mediation session may look like.

8. The RPM roster is drawn up and RPM begins. (Students wear their RPM badge and take a folder and pen out at playtime on their rostered day.)

9. The RPM coordinator schedules *phase 2 training* – regular ongoing meetings for RPMs to share their experiences, review difficult situations collectively, revise aspects of phase 1 training and receive additional training. Phase 2 training is the most important part of RPM training and is considered mandatory for RPMs.

The next section of this manual is the phase 1 training day that lays out the program for phase 1 training of your RPMs and the training booklet that the RPMs use during the day.

2

CIRCLES
How to Train Restorative Peer Mediators

Restorative processes (conferences) almost always take place in a circle, so it's fitting that your team of Restorative Peer Mediators (RPMs) will work together in circles during their phase 1 and 2 training.

Restorative practitioners understand the importance of building community amongst staff and students using circle processes. Schools simply do better when connection and belonging is enhanced through circles that promote dialogue, understanding, perspective taking, comradery and fun. Using circles pedagogy during the two phases of training will deliver these outcomes for your team of RPMs. It goes without saying that if we want our RPMs to engage in *emotionally literate ways* with the students whom they will be supporting in the yard, then we need to employ a pedagogy that teaches and encourages values that are congruent with this aim.

Circles in the broader context

Circles, traditionally known as 'Circle Time' and more recently 'Circle Solutions' (Roffey 2014), are used broadly in schools (particularly schools using Restorative Practices) as a centrepiece of their wellbeing programs to build understanding, trust and cohesion between groups of students and staff. Circles are also used in many schools as the preferred vehicle to deliver social and emotional learning (SEL), resilience programs, child protection curricula and content from mainstream academic subjects.

The communal nature of circles enhances learning because students are no longer only learning through direct instruction from a teacher, they are working in pairs, threes and entire class circles to share and reflect on their learning, hear others' perspectives on topics and think more deeply about content based on others' perspectives. The benefits of using circles are not limited to students however, school staff can tap into the benefits of working in circles to improve relationships with one another and utilize a range of circle processes to build shared understandings and make decisions together.

A school that is serious about teaching students skills for living and learning in a restorative school, where relationships are valued (and protected) above all else, need to use circles as the main way that people come together (into community) to enjoy each other's company, share experiences, understand each other's perspectives and continually work toward greater shared understandings of how each of us experience the world. The critical work that takes place in circles *greases the wheels* of social interaction and builds social capital:

> If the purpose of Restorative Practice is to restore relationships in the wake of wrongdoing or conflict, then the role of [circles]…is to help build the relationships children consider worth restoring. Circles are a practical way to skill young, developing human beings to listen with understanding, tune into feelings, share opinions and begin to see the world from another's viewpoint. These are the very skills children need to function successfully in any social setting. (Hansberry and Langley 2013, p.8)

ASPIRE principles circles

Roffey (2014) outlines six principles that underpin all interactions in circles and become the basis of the *circle guidelines* (rules), which are stated at the beginning of every circle session and sometimes during sessions to remind or re-focus students. The following are adapted from Roffey (2014, p.5), one of the best resources available for schools wishing to embed circles.

Below, each of these ASPIRE principles is outlined and explained in regards to how it relates to the training of the Restorative Peer Mediators (RPMs).

Agency

It is everybody's job in the circle to create a safe and positive atmosphere. Students work together in circles to build solutions to issues, rather than being told what to do by adults. Giving young people agency (the power to make decisions about things that affect them) helps change from an *external locus of control*, where everything is done *to* them or *for* them, to an *internal locus of control*, where young people learn that they can effect change. This sense of control is a key factor in building resilience.

Agency is an essential element of the training of RPMs, as the perspectives and ideas of the trainee RPMs are critical to the success of the RPM program in any school. When it comes to *what's happening* in any schoolyard, the perspective that counts most is the perspective of the students who occupy that space. The RPMs will know better than adults how to use what they learn in RPM training in their schoolyard. The different circle processes used in phase 1 and 2 training will draw this knowledge out and help the group find effective ways to use it in the day to day operation of the RPM program.

Safety and choice

In circles, nobody is pressured to speak and participants may 'pass' as often as they like. Teachers must not challenge this. By being in the circle, students are still watching, listening and learning from others. Most young people usually begin to contribute once they build up the confidence from watching others do this and see that it is safe to share.

Allowing the *right to pass* is often a challenging notion for teachers but with experience in circles they soon see that the vast majority of young people eventually take up the invitation to speak when it is their turn. During RPM training, we must accept that even though the young people training as RPMs have accepted a leadership position among peers, there will be parts of the RPM training where a young person may not have a perspective on a topic, might simply forget what they wanted to share with the group when their turn comes, or for whatever reason, may choose to withdraw from a conversation and exercise their right to pass.

With safety and choice in mind, the adult leading the training must accept this in that moment, and if they sense a deeper issue, they can quietly approach the student afterwards and enquire as to the reasons that they have passed or withdrawn from a group task.

Positivity

Circle activities deliberately trigger positive emotions. When people feel better about themselves and others they have more emotional resources to cope with challenge. (Fredrickson 2011, cited in Roffey 2014). An increased sense of belonging raises resilience. When there is a need to discuss an issue that is creating negative emotions within the group, the group becomes focused on seeking a solution. The focus of the group becomes: 'What will help us build an effective, inclusive, fair and happy team of RPMs?'

Inclusion

Everyone in the group is welcomed to the circle and is expected to work with all of the class or group. Mixing young people up so that they break out of their *cliques* and get to know one another better is a key feature of circles and young people accept this readily when an adult takes the time to explain this to them. I often ask groups of students, 'Why would someone like me ask you to play silly games that get you away from your normal friends and sitting with someone you might not know?' Even five-year-olds more often than not understand that this makes for safer schools! In training the RPMs, we are building a community of young people who have a common desire to help others in their school. Their effectiveness as RPMs will depend on how well they work together as they will be working interdependently.

Respect

In circles (and beyond), we respect what everyone has to say and the way in which we listen to each other matters. We are training RPMs to work respectfully with younger members of the school community, so they need to work respectfully with one another. Young people who experience respectful treatment are more likely to act respectfully towards others. This is a key aim for our RPMs.

Equality

There are equal opportunities to contribute. No one group or person is allowed to dominate. Knowing that everyone has their turn promotes cooperation. During RPM training equality is emphasized.

These ASPIRE principles become the basis of a very simple set of circle guidelines for circles that work well from early years through to adults:

- One person speaks at a time
- You can pass
- No put downs.

What does a circle look like?

Circles are an elegantly simple pedagogy, with each circle session following the same formula and operating by the same set of principles. The following has been adapted from Hansberry and Langley (2013).

How do people sit?

Everyone, including the adult leading the circle sits in a chair, in a circle. Teachers often ask if students can sit on the floor instead of chairs. In my experience, young people are able to maintain attention for longer when seated in chairs. Having everyone in chairs also keeps the shape of the circle, especially in mix-up games where people move to different seats to work with a new partner or grouping. In classes where students often sit on the floor, using chairs signifies the importance of *coming together* as a group in a circle.

Circle format

Some circle resource materials suggest an identical format each circle session. In phase 1 training, the different sections of the training follow a format similar to the one below:

1. Welcome by teacher and reminder of the guidelines for the circle
2. A quick energizer activity

3. A lively mix-up activity to get young people out of their typical social groups

4. The introduction of a skill, topic or question (*session theme*) for the group by the teacher

5. Paired or small group discussion in the topic or question and feedback to the circle by the pairs or groups

6. A whole group game or whole group skills practice activity

7. A concluding whole group activity.

Circle activities used in RPM training

Following is a summary of the different circle activity types used in the RPM trainings (phase 1 and 2). This, of course, is not an exhaustive list of circle activities, merely a selection of activities that we find best suit the purposes of training RPMs. A teacher who is experienced in using circles could make adaptations to the types of activities we've suggested to better suit their group and their own style of circle facilitation.

Reminder of the rules

The rules are revised at the beginning of every new circle session. Revisiting the agreed guidelines communicates how important it is that circles are a fun and safe place for all.

Energizers

These are activities like *pass the smile* (see page 34) that are lively and fun and begin to connect the circle. Energizers can be inserted at any point in the training when the facilitator senses that the circle has become *low on energy*.

Mix-up activities (change places games)

Mixing young people up so that they interact outside of normal social groups is fundamental to building an accepting and cohesive group. This is also a protective factor that inhibits the emergence of dominance-styled behaviours. *Change places games* are a popular way to get young people to move to different places in the circle. Be aware that it is completely normal for some children to try to sit next to their friends, even during RPM training. *Silent statements* is a mix-up activity used often in phase 1 RPM training to promote the sharing of opinions or information through movement.

Direct and explicit instruction

This is a time where the teacher talks about a main idea or theme and/or models a skill to the circle. The RPM training involves a particular set of skills based around using the *Restorative Peer Mediator Script* (see pages 113-114 and 127-128), so there are many parts of the training that involves explicit and direct instruction using the '*I do, we do, you do*' model.

Teacher comment

The teacher makes a brief comment to help children draw meaning from an activity, or points out what is similar or diverse about the responses once young people have shared something with the circle. Well-timed teacher comments help capture important teachable moments.

Pair share (partner activities)

This involves RPMs talking with a person sitting next to them to find something they have in common or something they agree on. This promotes questioning and listening.

Pair share with feedback

This is pair share, where partners share back what they discovered with the rest of the circle after talking to, or working with each other on a particular task. If information of a personal nature is to be shared with the larger circle, each partner should first ask the other permission to share what was discussed.

Go-around

The *talking piece* is passed around the circle, giving individual students, pairs or small groups the chance to share a thought, idea or complete a sentence. With practice and prompting, young people get better at keeping their responses brief and concise.

Story telling

The phase 1 training relies heavily on narratives (fictional scenarios) as the topic of all kinds of circle activities. These stories are read to the circle by the teacher and then the RPMs are set to work on a range of tasks in relation to the story.

Sentence completions

This is a go-around activity where the teacher provides a sentence starter and young people complete the sentence, sharing an opinion or feeling on a certain issue, for example, 'When I'm hurt, I need...' Each young person begins with 'When I'm hurt, I need' and then finishes the sentence with their response, for example, 'a friend to listen to me'. The teacher always begins the go-around.

Role plays

RPM's use role play scenarios (in small groups) to practice skills that have been modelled through direct instruction from the teacher. These are usually followed by feedback to the whole circle by the groups.

Circle brainstorm

All young people are invited to share ideas or thoughts by putting their hand up or standing up to indicate they have something to share. The teacher selects young people to share.

Is circle training for RPM teachers necessary?

In a word – yes! Circles is a pedagogy, based on a clear philosophy. In many ways, we need to remove our *teacher hat* when we facilitate circles. Otherwise, we run the risk of over-controlling sessions and facilitating in a way that is at odds with the philosophy of circles. This can send the wrong messages to young people about how to interact in circles. Undertaking training in circles facilitation gives teachers a much better chance of reaping the benefits of learning and relationships.

Where can I be trained in the Circle pedagogy?

Australia

- Hansberry Educational Consulting www.hansberryec.com.au

- Circle Solutions Network www.circlesolutionsnetwork.com

- Inyahead www.inyahead.com.au

- www.thorsborne.com.au/

United Kingdom

- Sue Rofley and Associates www.sueroffey.com

- Margaret Thorsborne and Associates

United States

- International Institute for Restorative Practices

Canada

- International Institute for Restorative Practices Canada
- https://canada.iirp.edu

New Zealand

- Restorative Schools
- www.restorativeschools.org.nz/training

3

PHASE 1 TRAINING DAY

The phase 1 training will take one (intensive) day with students who are already familiar with restorative process. For students who are new to peer mediation as well as being new to restorative practices, it is important to allocate an extra half day to the training program outlined in this section.

Students unfamiliar with restorative practices take longer to get their head around the principles and language of restorative practices, so extra time for explicit teaching and conversation in the circle is needed. They will also need more practice using the RPM scripts and process.

As mentioned previously, there is also the option of breaking the training into lessons and delivering the training through a learning unit as part of a health and personal development curriculum.

Suggested timetable for the training day

9:00am	Welcome
	Circle rules
	Warm-up (People Bingo)
	Section 1: Restorative Peer Mediation (RPM) – what is it?
Short Break	
9:45am	**Section 2:** Conflicts in our schoolyard
	Section 3: Paraphrasing
Morning Tea (provided)	
11:00am	**Section 4:** Understanding people's needs when they are hurt or have hurt others
	Section 5: Seeing things differently
	Section 6: Blaming and repairing
Lunch	
1:00pm	**Section 7a:** The RPM getting ready process and script: Early years and primary
	Section 7b: The RPM getting ready process and script: Upper primary, middle & secondary
	Section 8: Time to practise
	Section 9: Concluding circle

Introduction

Using circles to make your RPMs into a team

Welcome

Welcome to RPM training. I'm thrilled to be working with you all and really excited that you want to help the staff here to teach students to handle their friendship problems and conflicts in the yard.

A good team of RPMs will make life easier for our students and for our teachers as well.

Today will make you think hard. Just the same way we want to teach students in the yard to use their thinking brains to solve problems. We will all be tired at the end of the day, but will all be excited about the work we have done.

Circle rules

You might already know from circles in your own classrooms that there are some very important rules for circles.

Who knows these?

Great! We will use these today.

Pass the smile

Pass the smile is a fun activity where you (the trainer) begin with a smile and pass that smile to the person beside you by turning and smiling at them. The smile then travels around the circle and returns to you. This works best when you overemphasize the smile and pass on the biggest cheesiest grin you can!

> To warm us up, I'm going to pass a smile around our circle. Giving and getting smiles loosens everyone up and gets a good vibe going. When you are working as an RPM, smiling goes a long way to helping people feel better!
>
> Seeing a smile on a bigger person's face when younger kids are worried or sad relaxes their brains and their bodies so they are better able to fix problems.
>
> So, I'm going to turn and look at the person beside me and show them my biggest smile. That person is then going to turn and show the person beside them their biggest grin. We'll keep doing that until it gets right around the circle and back to me.

Warm-up

People Bingo

People Bingo will help the RPMs can get to know each other better. Some may not be familiar with each other and this game relaxes students who may be a little anxious about the training. It is good practice to involve yourself in the games and activities during the training day so that the students become familiar with you as well.

> Well, I'm feeling positive and ready to move on after watching those smiles go around the circle – thanks everyone!
>
> In your training manual you will find a game called 'People Bingo' (see pages 101 and 116). We are going to play this game to warm up, to get to know each other better and also to have a bit of fun.
>
> Your job is to fill in a person's name in every spot on the Bingo sheet. Here is the catch – you can only use each person once, so you will need to talk to many people and find out who matches each category.
>
> So, move around inside the circle talking to people and as soon as you have filled in each box with a different name, call out 'BINGO'.
>
> Is there anything I haven't explained well enough? – Ready, GO!

Sentence completion

It's important that students get to share with one another their reasons for wanting to be a RPM.

Great job with the Bingo everyone! I hope that you learnt a little more about other RPMs and that you had a bit of fun, too! I know I learnt lots about you all!

Before we complete the next activity, can we please, in a go-around, complete this sentence:

'I chose to become an RPM because...'

Section 1: Restorative Peer Mediation (RPM) – What is it?

Mix-up and pair share

Opposites cards, find your match

To build a more cohesive group in any situation where a sense of teamwork is needed, it's important to mix students up regularly. This is a simple mix-up activity where students are given an 'opposites card' (see Appendix 1).

The task for group members is to find the holder of their card's opposite without making a sound. Once they locate the holder of their card's opposite, they take a seat in the circle next to their partner.

Hand out the *opposite cards* and once the pairs have formed and settled in seats, get them thinking and talking with each other about what they think Restorative Peer Mediation is.

> With your new partner, I would like you to talk about what you believe *Restorative Peer Mediation* is all about.
>
> You've got three minutes to both agree on two ideas. Be ready to feed back your combined thoughts to the rest of the group.

When the students have had three minutes talking time, have them feed back their responses to the circle. Record these on a large sheet of paper.

For repeated responses – just tick the response to indicate that it was said again.

That's an amazing list! As you can see, working as a Restorative Peer Mediator is a complex and important job.

Now, turn to the person on the other side of you in the circle. Your task is to look at what is recorded here [motion toward the responses from the previous task] and to see if you can create a *definition* of what a Restorative Peer Mediator is.

To help you create your definition, choose what you agree are the *most important words* from what we have here [on the large piece of paper] to include.

You have three minutes. In your training manual, there is a space to write your definition under the heading, *'Our Definition of an RPM'* (see pages 102 and 117).

When the time is up, ask for pairs that would like to read out their definition – not all pairs need to.

Circle or highlight key words from the previous brainstormed list as they read their definitions.

There are some excellent definitions there – well done!

In your training manual, there is a space for you to write a definition of what a Restorative Peer Mediator is. It's under the heading *'My Definition of an RPM'* (see pages 103 and 118).

You may choose to either write *your own definition* or, if you like, *another group's definition* better than your own, you can use theirs. You don't have to use the same definition as your partner.

Take three minutes to write your definition in the box.

Section 2: Conflicts in our schoolyard

Pair share

NOTE: If training students from multiple schools, students will need to be in same school groups for this activity.

Every school differs in the nature of conflicts that take place in the schoolyard. An early years friendship issue will be very different to a Year 9 friendship problem!

In this activity, we ask the RPMs to come up with a list of *common types of conflict* that they have seen in the yard at their school.

This list will spark conversation about the types of conflicts that are appropriate to be handled by an RPM and those that should be referred to a member of staff. It will also create a list of conflicts that can be used later in the training where the RPMs practise using the scripted restorative questions.

Before you begin this section – mix students up again in the circle. You could use the suggestions below, or choose your own.

Change places if:

- You have shoes with laces
- You have brown eyes
- You try to be a good listener.

> As you already know, when kids are together at recess and lunchtimes, things go wrong sometimes! Students can get upset with each other for many different reasons.
>
> I want you to think about your/our school and the types of conflicts that you've seen or heard about in the yard.
>
> Talk to your new partner and come up with two conflict situations from the yard that you think an RPM would be able to help sort out.
>
> Then, come up with one conflict situation that you think RPMs would definitely let a staff member handle. Be ready to feed these back to the circle.

Record each pair's responses on a large sheet to be used later. As students feed back their responses, ensure that they are appropriate for RPMs to deal with.

Have a separate column for conflicts that would *not be appropriate* (e.g., on-going family feuds, physical violence, on-going bullying behaviour, injuries, etc.)

RPMs should then write some of the most common conflicts into their training manual under the heading 'Conflicts in Our Schoolyard' (see pages 104 and 119).

Section 3: Paraphrasing

I'm about to show you one skill that great conference facilitators, counsellors and even psychologists use. As well as helping you as a peer mediator, it's also a skill that will make you an excellent conversationalist.

When you use this skill, people want to talk to you more often! It's a skill that most of you would use already but might not know you are using it.

Now, close your manuals and put them under your seats.

I need a volunteer from the circle to talk to me (in front of the rest of the circle) about their favourite pet, app, sport or YouTube celebrity. I need someone who can talk for about 30 seconds.

Can I have a volunteer?

What are you going to talk to me about? Great!

Can you leave the area for a moment and decide what you want me to know about your favourite thing?

Say to the rest of the circle:

When [insert volunteer's name] comes back and begins to tell me about their [insert topic] I will try to use this skill I've been talking about.

Your job is to listen carefully and see if you can work out what skill I'm using as I listen. It's a particular listening skill.

Call the volunteer talker back into the circle.

What comes next can be done with you both sitting in your normal seats in the circle, or standing or sitting in chairs in the middle of the circle. If you decide to use the middle of the circle, be aware that there will be students who won't be able to see your faces.

Ask the volunteer to begin talking to you about their chosen subject. As they speak, use paraphrasing.

The key component skills to model to the RPMs are:

1. Look at the speaker's face as they talk.

2. **Wait for pauses** in their story and

3. **Briefly repeat** (paraphrase) in your own words the **most important parts** of what they have just said.

   i. Paraphrases can be just a few words or one or two brief sentences.

   ii. You will know the most important parts of what they tell you because they will show the most emotion (seem **happiest** or **saddest**) as they say them – these are the bits of the story with the **strongest emotions** attached to them. So, watch their face carefully and listen to their voice.

4. **Watch the student's face** after you have paraphrased. If they look at your eyes and seem pleased with what you have said or agree with what you just said, then it worked. If they look confused, look downward or grumpy, or stop talking, say, 'Sorry, I interrupted you, keep telling me about it.'

Thank your volunteer and then ask them quietly if they think they have worked out what the skill you were using was but ask them to keep it to themselves for a moment while the pairs do a **pair share** to see if they can agree what the skill was.

Change places

Okay, Restorative Peer Mediators:

- Change places if you think you can name the skill I was using

- Change places again if you think you know why a peer mediator would use this skill

- Change places if you have laces on your shoes.

Pair share and feedback

Pair off around the circle and say 'Hi' to your new partner.

Take 60 seconds to see if you can both agree on which skill I was demonstrating. Be ready to share back with the circle at the end.

After a minute (or two):

Okay, let's go around the circle and hear from pairs what they think the skill is.

Pairs will mention many things they observed you doing, such as:

- Giving eye contact
- Nodding
- Looking interested
- Smiling
- Repeating back what was said.

As pairs share their guesses with the circle, thank them for their thoughts and speak kindly about all suggestions.

At the conclusion of the go-around say:

> You identified lots of things I did and many of you picked up exactly how I *repeated back in words and short sentences that [volunteer's name] said*, especially the parts that he/she seemed most excited about.
>
> So, why might *paraphrasing* be helpful to an RPM when helping other students in the yard?

Invite suggestions from the circle.

Practice time

> Paraphrasing is about picking just the right time to say things that show that you're understanding someone's story, but, at the same time, you're not interrupting them.
>
> Here are the steps for paraphrasing – you can find them in your training manual (see pages 105 and 120).

How to do great paraphrasing:

1. Look and listen to the person talking

2. **Wait for a pause** in what they are saying and

3. **Say back** in just a few words the **most important parts** of what they have just said:

   » So you felt...

   » They were...

   » It was...

   » You were...

Turn to your partner and let's have a go at this skill of paraphrasing.

I want you to take turns to tell one another what's been the most memorable part of today's learning so far – the bit that has stuck in your mind.

If you can't think of something that has been memorable from today, tell your partner about your favourite movie, a pet or your bedroom!

When it is your turn to listen, you will practise waiting for pauses, and saying back, in a few words, or a short sentence, what your partner has said to you.

Take a moment to think about what you might talk about, then decide with your partner on who will listen first.

Give pairs a couple of minutes to share with one another and practise paraphrasing. Move around the circle and observe.

When pairs look as though they are winding down:

Watching you all do this for the first time was incredible. You're already experts. I think you are so good at this that you could use paraphrasing the next time your parents are telling you off for something!

Change places and pair share and feedback

> Now, quickly change places in the circle if you are wearing something with black on it.
>
> Say 'Hi' to your new partner and chat with them about these questions:
>
> - How did it feel to have someone paraphrasing you?
>
> - What was good about being paraphrased – when did it work well?
>
> - What was not good about being paraphrased – when didn't it work well?
>
> Be ready to share back to the circle:
>
> - One thing you agreed that made paraphrasing work well and how you knew this
>
> - One thing that you agreed ruined it and how you knew this.

In this activity, you want students to discover for themselves what makes paraphrasing work well and what spoils it!

As pairs share back responses to the circle, ask, 'How did you know that it was working well/not working well?'

You are trying to help students see that paraphrasing is working well when the other person:

- Looks up at you for a second after you paraphrase

- Keeps talking with even more enthusiasm after you have paraphrased

- Nods, smiles or does something else to show that they like what you said.

And that you are might doing too much paraphrasing when the other person:

- Stops and goes quiet

- Shakes their head

- Looks angry or irritated after you paraphrase

- Says something like, 'Don't interrupt me!'

Refer students to their training manual where this information is summarized (see pages 102 and 105).

RPMs will discover that:

- Trying to paraphrase **too much** sounds like interrupting and is frustrating for the person talking.

- Making your paraphrases **too long** makes it seem as though you have taken over and this will stop the other person talking

- You should **never begin telling your own story** when you're supposed to be the one listening.

So, we've learned that:

- Too much paraphrasing frustrates people

- We need to keep paraphrases short so it doesn't feel like we are interrupting

- We should NEVER let a paraphrase turn into us telling our own story about something – our job is to listen.

Great job team! That's great advice.

We also know that our paraphrasing is working if a person:

- Looks up briefly

- Nods or smiles

- Keeps talking.

We know that it's not working if a person:

- Stops and goes quiet

- Shakes their head or looks grumpy

- Looks angry or irritated after you paraphrase.

Take the next two minutes to talk with your partner about where else (besides in peer mediation) you might use paraphrasing.

As you listen to your partner, keep practising paraphrasing and watching their reaction to your paraphrasing carefully.

Use paraphrasing with your parents the next time they are telling you off about something! See what happens!

Section 4: Understanding people's needs when they are hurt or have hurt others

Suitable for all RPMs

Materials needed

- Pictures from Appendix 13 of the 'Grab and Go Circle Time Kit' (Hansberry and Langley 2013), cut into halves to be matched to form pairs

- Talking piece

Mix-up activity to create pairs

Spread cut-up pictures from Appendix 13 of the 'Grab and Go Circle Time Kit' (Hansberry and Langley 2013) out on the floor.

Alternatively, play a mix-up game to create pairs. However, using the 'conflict picture cards' (the cut up pictures) to form pairs will prime students to begin thinking about the feelings and needs that harm and conflict create.

> On the floor are picture halves. When I say, 'Go!', pick up a picture half and then find someone who has the matching other half of your picture. Sit next to them in the circle.

This is the point in the training where RPMs begin to realise that an important part of restorative mediation is to *bring affected students together* so they can talk with each other about what happened, who is upset or hurt and what will make the situation better. When students are brought together to talk in this way, the needs created have a much better chance of being taken care of.

TEACHER INFORMATION

Affect Script Psychology[1] teaches us that when a restorative process is managed correctly, the people involved in the problem become each other's best source of relief from the awful thoughts and feelings created by the problem. This is why it is important to bring students together to try to sort the issue out rather than attempting to broker a solution by talking to students in isolation. With an understanding of the emotional dynamics in restorative conferencing, you can explain this to the RPMs. You can find out more about this in Chapters 1 and 2 of *The Psychology of Emotion in Restorative Practice* (Thorsborne and Kelly 2014).

With older students, you may wish to teach them about The Compass of Shame as it brings incredible insight into why people do what they do when in conflict (Hansberry 2016).[2]

Give new pairs a moment to chat and settle in. Then say to the circle:

When people get into a mess with each other, like in a conflict, or when someone is hurt by the actions of another, everyone involved in the problem will have needs that must be taken care of so the problem can be sorted out.

When helping people with their conflicts, it's easy to spend too long talking to the person we think did the wrong thing, or the opposite: just listening to the person who looks most upset.

We need to balance our care.

---

1   Affect Script Psychology, developed by the psychologist Silvan Tomkins, is a theory of human emotion and motivation that explains that all human emotion originates from nine biological inborn programs (affects). This elegant but complex theory fills many gaps left by Freudian theory and has been embraced by the Restorative Practices community as a framework for explaining the emotional dynamics at work in Restorative Practice.

2   The Compass of Shame is a powerful model, first developed by Donald Nathanson MD, that explains four universal sets of unhelpful behaviours (*withdrawal*, *attack-self*, *avoidance* and *attack-other*) that humans use to try to make painful feelings of shame go away when we cannot deal constructively with them.

The Soccer Story

Suitable for all RPMs

The Soccer Story is a carefully chosen case study that works well with RPMs whether they will be working with young primary-aged students or middle school students. Older students come to understand that even though the details of this incident in this story involve younger kids with immature behaviours, the emotions involved (jealousy, embarrassment (shame), anger, worry) are just the same, regardless of the age of students involved.

If you are concerned about the relevance of this story to older students, consider using *The Basketball Story* (on pages 55 and 122). If you have time, you can use both stories and complete the different needs activities (that follow) with both stories.

> To work out what needs we have when hurt, or when we have caused harm, I want to share a story with you.
>
> This story includes a serious incident that within a primary school, a teacher would usually need to deal with. I am using it as an example so that you might be able to put yourself in this position and imagine what feelings the people involved in the story might have.
>
> As an RPM you will often come across situations similar to this, without the physical harm. The story is in your training manual. Feel free to read along silently with me as I read, or just sit back and listen to me as I read it.

THE SOCCER STORY

(From *The Grab and Go Circle Time Kit for Teaching Restorative Behaviour* (Hansberry and Langley 2013).)

Pete, John and Lance were playing with a soccer ball at recess time. They were taking turns to try to kick the ball into the goals. It was Pete's turn. John and Lance stood in front of goals as the two goal keepers– it was their job to try to stop the ball going through when Pete kicked it.

Pete was the only one who hadn't scored a goal. John and Lance had kicked a goal each. Pete was worried that he'd be the only one who hadn't kicked a goal. He didn't want to look like a bad soccer player.

Pete took a big run-up and kicked as hard as he could. The ball went flying through the air toward the goals – it was a great kick and looked as though it would be a goal for sure. Lance knew he'd have to jump as high as he could to stop the goal. He shut his eyes and jumped with his arms outstretched as high as he could.

The ball just touched the tips of his fingers and then flew over the top of the goals. Lance and his tremendous leap had just stopped a certain goal! When Pete saw that Lance had stopped the goal, his face turned to thunder. He thought to himself, 'The bell is going and I'm the only one who hasn't scored a goal.' He felt his stomach tighten into a knot and his face get really hot. His feelings were taking control of him.

Pete picked up a lump of dirt and threw it at Lance. It hit Lance right in the face. Lance fell to the ground with dirt in his eyes and started to cry. John yelled angrily at Pete 'Why did you do that?' Pete didn't know why he'd just hurt Lance. His brain felt like scrambled eggs and he couldn't think of anything to say. Pete felt angry at himself and wished he could undo what he just did. Lance went to the sick room and Pete went to the office.

Change places

Poor Lance; getting dirt thrown in his face.

Swap seats if:

- You have seen someone be hurt or treated badly

- You have felt upset when someone did something unkind or mean to another person.

Pair share: Lance's needs

Pair RPMs off around the circle (or into small groups).

Let's use what we know about needs and imagine that you were Lance. What would you need to feel better?

Take a moment to talk with the person next to you about what Lance would need immediately, and then later. Agree on two things and be ready to share.

Go-around: Lance's needs

When I pass the Talking Piece around the circle, can each person share one of the things you agreed on?

Record ideas on a large sheet of paper – these will be used later.

That's a terrific list of suggestions to meet some of Lance's needs. We have [read list of ideas].

Now, think for a moment about a time when you have been hurt and what someone did to help you feel better.

What else can we add to our list? When you think of an idea, put your hand up and I'll roll you the ball. You can only speak when you have the ball. When you have shared, roll the ball to someone else.

Wow! So, now we have a great list of all our ideas about what people need to feel better when they are hurt. If we know what people need to feel better when they are hurt, this might help us help them sort out the problem?

Pair share: Pete's needs

> Take a moment to talk with the person next to you about what Pete would need straight away, and then later. Agree on two things and be ready to share.

Go-around: Pete's needs

> When I pass the Talking Piece around the circle, can each of you share one of the things you agreed on?

Record ideas on a large sheet of paper – these will be used later.

When *revenge* comes up!

Occasionally, vengeful acts may be suggested. This might come in the form of humour, but resist the temptation to dismiss this type of response. Respectfully accept these suggestions, they need airing. It's well worth taking a few minutes to explore this with the group. The insight will be truly unexpected and delightful. Pose these questions to the group as a pair share and feedback, a go-around, or just as open conversation:

'It's true, thoughts of revenge do make us feel better in the first instance,' or 'Doing the same to them can feel good for a little while can't it?' 'Did you know that revenge is a very normal impulse in humans?'

- What is it about payback that feels so good for some people?

- When payback happens, what are the feelings on both sides – the person doing the payback and the recipient?

- What normally happens after payback? Does the person say, 'Oh, thanks for paying me back, now I know how you must have felt and I'll never do that again?'

- What happens to the friendships of people who use payback often?

- Did you know the urge for revenge comes from a part of the brain called the Caudate Nucleus?

TEACHER INFORMATION

Neurologically speaking, the very normal urge to seek revenge when an injustice has been perceived can be linked to a cluster of neurones in the centre of the human brain called the Caudate Nucleus. Modern brain scanning techniques (fMRI) have shown that the Caudate Nucleus becomes active when we have thoughts of revenge. This very same part of the brain also lights up when we think of something we like to eat, like chocolate cake. Revenge is in fact sweet! This is of course simplifying a very complex system of low road (unconscious) neural systems, but is interesting to note nevertheless! Our role as teachers is to firstly override our innate desire for revenge when students do the wrong thing (tit-for-tat impulses), and to help students to do the same. The educative (teaching) component of discipline is very quickly lost in schools and classrooms where tit-for-tat cycles of revenge (retributive justice) dominate student interactions and disciplinary processes. (Hansberry 2009, p.18)

Identifying a commonality of needs

You will now have two columns on the paper – one side for Lance's needs and the other for Pete's needs. You will notice that Lance and Pete will have some needs in common, including:

- Both needing to have their story heard

- Both needing to be taken care of straight after the incident

- Both needing some space initially to come to terms with the incident

- Both needing comfort.

With a little interpretation of the suggestions made by the pairs, it will be easy for the RPMs to spot needs that Lance and Pete have in common, even though one of them was the *perpetrator* of the incident and one was the *innocent victim*!

> Looking at the two lists here, what needs can you see that both boys share?
>
> Hands up when you spot something.

> One of the ways that Restorative Practice is a little different to other ways of thinking about problems is that it acknowledges that when things go wrong, needs are created on both sides – on the side of the person who had the 'ouch' (Lance) and the 'oops' person (Pete). Well done on noticing this.

Pass the main idea

> That was great work RPMs. In a moment, we are going to pass a hi-5 around the circle but we will also pass something else. To help lock in our learning, we will pass the main idea we got from the activities we just did.
>
> Take a moment to decide what you think the most important piece of learning about people's needs when they are hurt or caused hurt was. Keep it to just a few words.
>
> Now, when you pass the hi-5, tell the person what your most important learning was. I'll begin.

RPMs can record what they believe the most important needs are in their training manual (see pages 108 and 124). This will help them remember the rich conversations and learning when they are re-reading their notes from the training day down the track.

★

Alternative story – Go away, Jessica

Following is a story that can be used instead of *The Soccer Story* or in addition to it, if time permits. This scenario involves more subtle harmful behaviour that is more often observed in girls as they begin to experiment with social power. Following this story, as with *The Soccer Story*, ask the RPMs to identify the needs of all of the characters and then look for common needs that Jessica, Sarah and Violet share in the wake of the incident.

▨ GO AWAY, JESSICA

Sarah, Violet and Jessica were all in Mrs Justice's grade 1 class. Sarah and Violet were family friends and had spent the previous weekend camping together. At lunch time, they were eating their vegemite sandwiches and laughing about how much fun the camping trip was and how funny it was when Sarah's brother Andrew had fallen off of his bike into a muddy puddle and had mud all over his face.

Jessica, who hadn't been on the trip with Saran and Violet, was standing next to the girls and feeling a little left out of the conversation because Sarah and Violet had turned their backs on her as they talked about the weekend. 'Hey, let's go and play on the monkey bars,' said Jessica.

'We're talking about camping,' said Violet.

'Only people who came camping on the weekend can play with us today,' said Sarah with a mean grin on her face.

'We will tell you when you can play with us,' added Violet.

Jessica felt very sad because she knew what Violet and Sarah were doing was unkind and was against the school values of inclusion. Inclusion was something that they had been learning about in their class. Jessica, in her best assertive voice, said, 'That's not very nice, we have to include each other.'

'Go away, Jessica,' said Sarah sharply.

Jessica was feeling angry and confused all at once. Violet and Sarah were her friends and they usually played together and were kind to one another. Today was very different and she didn't know why the girls were leaving her out. She also knew what they were doing was wrong because it was mean. Jessica didn't want Violet and Sarah to get into trouble but did want to get some help from an RPM. She walked away from Sarah and Violet, trying not to cry.

Sarah felt annoyed at Jessica for telling her that what she was doing wasn't nice but also she felt guilty for telling Jessica to go away. 'I'm not normally mean to people,' she thought to herself. Even though she felt bad about how she'd treated Jessica, she didn't fix the problem. She just watched as Jessica walked away.

Violet knew that Jessica's feelings had been hurt and wondered why Sarah had been so mean to Jessica. Violet wanted to play with Jessica, but only once she and Sarah had finished talking about the camping trip. She didn't tell Sarah that she thought this. Violet was worried that Jessica wouldn't want to be her friend anymore and was upset with Sarah for telling Jessica to go away in such a mean way.

★

Alternative story – The Basketball Story
For RPMs who will be working with older students

The Basketball Story below is similar to *The Soccer Story* in that it discusses the same emotions that fuelled Pete's behaviour (shame, jealousy and competitiveness). It can be used at this point as an option and the same needs identification activities that followed *The Soccer Story* can be used (if time permits).

If this story is used *in addition* to *The Soccer Story*, RPMs will discover that the emotions felt by the boys and needs created by incident are the same, even though the boys involved are older in this second scenario and the behaviours are different.

To work out what needs we have when hurt, or when we have caused harm, I want to share a story with you.

This story includes an incident that took place in a secondary school.

As an RPM, you will often come across situations similar to this, the story is in your training manual (see pages 48 and 122). Feel free to read along silently with me as I read, or just sit back and listen to me as I read it.

THE BASKETBALL STORY

Now, imagine that Lance, Pete and John aren't little kids; they are now 13-year-olds playing a game of around the world at the basketball courts.

John, Lance and Pete were playing a game of around the world on the basketball courts. It was a game where the winner was the first to sink a shot from different places on the court and finally a long shot. If a person scored, they moved to the next place for a bonus shot. If they missed, it was the next person's go. The winner finished first.

John had already shot and scored from all places so it was down to Lance and Pete. They were both on the long shot spot and the first to sink it would come in 2nd place. Pete had come last in the last two games and was starting to feel pretty uptight about the prospect of coming last again. There'd been some friendly trash talk between the boys and Pete was getting edgy as Lance got ready to shoot his pong shot. If Lance hit the shot, Pete was going to be last...again.

Lance looked at Pete, winked at him and said, 'Game over, bitch.' He shot the ball. It looked perfectly straight out of his hand. It sailed through the air on the perfect arc and then, swish! Nothing but net.

Lance turned to Pete and shouted, 'Yeah!' as he pumped his fist in the air close to Pete's face. Pete felt a wave of anger wash over him. His jaw clenched and his shoulders pulled back. Pete eyeballed Lance and said, 'You shoot well for a guy with a retard for a mum.'

This was a bad enough thing to say to someone but what made it worse was that Lance's mother had recently been diagnosed with Multiple Sclerosis. Pete knew this and, in his embarrassment about coming last, he made an insult of it. He had crossed the line. This wasn't banter; it was one of the worst things you could say to someone.

Lance couldn't believe what Pete had just said. He froze to the spot, wide eyed. His mouth hung open. After a moment, John said to Pete, 'Dude, that was unnecessary.' Pete felt sick about his cruel and jealous comment but instead of admitting he was wrong, he said, 'That's what you get if you get up in my face.' John just shook his head. Pete knew he had crossed a line that should never be crossed. Insulting someone's mum was bad enough, but to make an insult about a serious illness was unspeakable. He wished he could take it back. Lance was fighting back tears. He was so ashamed, even though he was the victim of Pete's comment.

Lance wanted to run at Pete and knock him down to defend his mum's honour, but he knew Pete was stronger than him. He took a deep breath and then said to Pete, 'I'm getting an RPM before I decide to cave your head in.'

Section 5: Seeing things differently

Many young children believe that everyone sees the world just as they do. This is known as 'egocentricity' and most young people grow out of it. There are, however, many students who, for a range of developmental or mental health reasons, remain egocentric and struggle to understand the needs, wants and desires of others.

To be able to be good RPMs it's important to know that sometimes you will have two people who saw the same event but have a completely different story. When asking 'What happened?' we often hear another person say things that we don't believe happened.

We often automatically think that someone is lying. Sometimes, this is the case, but not as often as you'd think.

One of the ways that Restorative Practice is a little different to other ways of thinking about problems is that it acknowledges that when things go wrong, needs are created on both sides – on the side of the person who had the 'ouch' (Lance) and the 'oops' person (Pete). Well done on noticing this.

Story: The Six Blind Men and the Elephant
Suitable for all RPMs

> I'm going to tell a story about six blind men and an elephant. This is a funny story because all of the men in this story thought they were telling the truth but all of their stories were different!
>
> This story is in your training manual (see pages 111 and 126). Feel free to read along silently with me as I read, or just sit back and listen to me as I read.

▨ THE SIX BLIND MEN AND THE ELEPHANT[3] ▨

Once upon a time, there lived six blind men in a village. Being blind meant that their eyes didn't work properly and they couldn't see. One day, the villagers told them, 'Hey, there is an elephant in the village today.'

The six blind men had no idea what an elephant was. They decided, 'Even though we will not be able to see it, let's go and feel it anyway.' All of them went to where the elephant was. Each of them touched the elephant.

'Hey, the elephant is like a pillar that holds a large building up,' said the first man, who touched the elephant's leg.

'No! It is like a rope,' said the second man, who touched the tail.

'No! It is like a thick branch of a tree,' said the third man, who touched the trunk of the elephant.

'It is like a big hand fan,' said the fourth man, who touched the ear of the elephant.

'It is like a huge wall,' said the fifth man, who touched the side of the elephant.

'It is like a solid pipe,' said the sixth man, who touched the tusk of the elephant.

They began to argue about the elephant and every one of them insisted that he was right. The six men were getting angry with one another.

A wise man was passing by and he saw this. He stopped and asked them, 'What is the matter?' They said, 'We cannot agree on what the elephant is like.' Each one of them said what he thought the elephant was like. The wise man calmly explained to them, 'All of you are right. The reason every

---

3   For an animated version, go to: www.youtube.com/watch?v=Vn9BUfUCL4I.

one of you is telling it differently because you all felt a different part of the elephant. So, the elephant is like all of the things you said.'

'Oh!' the six blind men said. There was no more fighting. The six blind men felt happy that they were all right.

The moral of the story is that there may be some truth to what someone says, even if their story is different to ours. So, instead of arguing like the blind men, we can say, 'Maybe you saw it differently to me.' This way, we don't get in as many arguments.

Circle brainstorm/Ball throw

That was an interesting story. Who would like to share what they were thinking while I was reading that story?

Who would like to share what they were thinking at the end of the story?

Why do you think I told that story?

How does that story apply to our work as RPMs?

Section 6: Blaming and repairing

Suitable for all RPMs

TEACHER INFORMATION

Story telling, listening and understanding become commonplace in schools that use restorative processes as a first approach to problems. Alternatively, punitive schools create punitive students. If blame and punishment are commonplace responses to wrongdoing and conflict, children soon fall into line with the prevailing culture.

This part of the training explores the different outcomes that are achieved when the goal of any response to wrongdoing or conflict is to look for solutions rather than finding out who should be blamed for what went wrong.

Play 'what if'

Pose the following questions to the circle, or do as an activity in pairs:

- *What if* Pete was sent to yard time out and Lance went to the sick room and they weren't brought together again to talk about what happened?

- Looking back at our list of what Pete and Lance both need, are their needs being met? Why or why not?

- What would it be like for them next time they would be together?

- *What if* the boys didn't get any help at all?

Modelling the Restorative Process for work with younger students

For RPMs who will be working with early years students

This section explains how the trainer can model the RPM process for younger students to trainee RPMs. The teacher uses the RPM Getting Ready Process and Script for Early Years (see page 111).

Getting kids ready to do restorative work

Ask all RPMs to open their training manuals to page 111 so they can see their RPM Getting Ready Process.

Half the job when working with people who are upset is to get them ready to meet to talk with each other about the problem. This can be the trickiest part because this is where we make decisions about whether the problem needs to be mediated, whether we need to refer the problem to a teacher and if we do go ahead, we need to work out who needs to be involved in the mediation and where to do the mediation!

We are going to have a close look at using the Getting Ready Process a little later (Section 7a).

Building empathy

The next activity is a perspective taking and empathy building task. Don't tell the students what is coming next; it will detract from the spontaneity of the activity. Begin this activity by dividing the students into two groups – two halves of the circle.

One half of the circle will now become the thoughts and feelings of Lance. They need to think about what happened from his point of view.

The other half of the circle will become the thoughts and feelings of Pete. They need to think about what happened from his point of view.

Take two minutes to form smaller circles in your groups and try to agree on what your character will be *feeling*, *thinking* and *needing* after the incident. Be ready to share this in the next activity.

TEACHER INFORMATION

As the teacher, you are now going to model to the RPMs how asking restorative questions to students (in front of one another) is a very important aspect of restoring relationships and repairing harm. As the teacher, you will recognize the scripted restorative questions, but the purpose of this activity is only to show the RPMs the power of getting students talking and listening to one another, as opposed to dealing with them separately and trying to get resolution without dialogue between the children involved.

Hi boys. It's great that you are both prepared and ready to participate in a restorative chat. Lance, you came to me with a problem that you are worried about.

Pete, Lance said you will be able to help us fix the problem. Will you help us? Great!

Our three rules are: Be respectful, be honest and take turns to speak.

Will you all follow these rules?

That's great, this shouldn't take long then.

Pete, what happened?

[Paraphrase the response]

Encourage the students on the *Pete* and *Lance* halves of the circle to respond, as their character, to the questions as you ask them.

The two different groups representing Lance and Pete will debate among themselves how to respond to the questions that you ask of them. This could get loud and energetic! This is important because they will be actively engaged in considering and predicting the different responses that could come from students in Lance and Pete's situation.

The RPMs will be *perspective taking*, using *empathic understanding* as well as thinking about what you've taught them about the *needs* that arise from these types of problems. This is just the type of thinking we want them to be doing.

★

TEACHER INFORMATION

This type of perspective taking may be a significant challenge for some students, particularly those with Autistic Spectrum Disorder, where mind blindness is a typical part of the cluster of their social comprehension difficulties.

You may wish to ask groups to agree on a particular response, or allow the different possible responses to come freely from different members of each group (like a brainstorm).

Judge whether a more or less structured approach works best for the groups, or ask them before beginning the activity how they think it might work best and what should happen if they find that the way they have chosen to run the activity isn't working well.

Lance, what happened from your side?

[Paraphrase the response]

Your skills as a restorative facilitator will be on show as you model how to keep the process on track by using the script questions, but also remain responsive to Lance and Pete's responses.

As you ask the remaining scripted questions to Lance and Pete, stick as closely as you can to the script that you will later be teaching the RPMs.

Pete, when you threw dirt at Lance, was that fair or unfair?

[Paraphrase response: 'You think it was...']

Lance, how are you feeling after having had dirt thrown at your face?

[Paraphrase response: *'You're feeling...'*]

Lance, what can we do to fix this problem?

[Paraphrase response: *'So you think...'*]

Pete, what do you think of Lance's idea?

[Paraphrase response]

So, you both think that [insert appropriate statement based on their responses] needs to happen to fix this problem.

Can you do this on your own or would you like some help?

Thanks for letting me help you sort this out. Let's finish with a hi-5.

Silent statements

> Change places if:
>
> - There are different feelings now in your group to what there were when we started
>
> - If your character (Lance or Pete) would be feeling better now than he was before the questions
>
> - If you believe that having a chance to answer the questions that I just asked would meet some of the needs we discussed earlier.

Encourage further conversation in the circle about how Lance and Pete might be feeling now after being asked these questions.

Modelling the Restorative Process for work with older students
Suitable for RPMs who will be working with upper primary, middle and secondary students

This part of the section explains how the trainer can model the RPM process for older students to trainee RPMs. The teacher uses *the RPM Getting Ready Process and Script* for RPMs working with older primary, middle and secondary students.

TEACHER INFORMATION

As the teacher, you are now going to model to the RPMs how asking restorative questions to students questions (in front of one another) is a very important aspect of restoring relationships and repairing harm. As the teacher, you will recognize the scripted restorative questions, but the purpose of this activity is only to show the RPMs the power of getting students talking and listening to one another, as opposed to dealing with them separately and trying to get resolution without dialogue between the involved children.

Hi, I'm [name] and I'm an RPM. It's my job to help people sort out problems. Lance told me about a problem that he would like to sort out with you. He said they didn't want to make a big deal of it and didn't think teachers needed to be involved yet. Are you interested in solving the problem?

Do you agree to be respectful, be honest and take turns to speak? Will you all follow these rules?

That's great, this shouldn't take long then.

Pete, what happened?

[Paraphrase the response.]

Encourage the students on the *Pete* and *Lance* halves of the circle to respond, as their character, to the questions as you ask them.

The two different groups representing Lance and Pete will debate among themselves about how to respond to the questions that you ask of them. This could get loud and energetic! This is important because they will be actively engaged in considering and predicting the different responses that could come from students in Lance and Pete's situation.

The RPMs will be *perspective taking*, using *empathic understanding* as well as thinking about what you've taught them about the *needs* that arise from these types of problems. This is just the type of thinking we want them to be doing.

TEACHER INFORMATION

This type of perspective taking may be a significant challenge for some students, particularly those with Autistic Spectrum Disorder, where mind blindness is a typical part of the cluster of their social comprehension difficulties.

You may wish to ask groups to agree on a particular response, or allow the different possible responses to come freely from different members of each group (like a brainstorm).

Judge whether a more or less structured approach works best for the groups, or ask them before beginning the activity how they think it might work best and what should happen if they find that the way they have chosen to run the activity isn't working well.

Lance, what happened from your side?

[Paraphrase the response.]

Your skills as a restorative facilitator will be on show as you model how to keep the process on track by using the script questions, but also remain responsive to Lance and Pete's responses.

As you ask the remaining scripted questions to Lance and Pete, stick as closely as you can to the script that you will later be teaching the RPMs.

Pete, what were you hoping would happen when you said that about Lance's mum?

Was saying that fair or unfair?

[Paraphrase response.]

Lance, how did hearing Pete say that affect you?

[Paraphrase Lance's response.]

Lance, what can we do to fix this problem?

[Paraphrase response: 'So you think...']

Pete, what do you think of Lance's idea?

[Paraphrase response.]

So, to fix this problem, you have agreed to [insert statements based on their conversation]. Pete, what's your part in this? Lance, how about you?

Is there anything anyone wants to add, or say to the other before we finish?

Thanks for letting me help you sort this out.

Silent statements

Change places if:

- There are different feelings now in your group to what there were when we started

- Your character (Lance or Pete) would be feeling better now that he was before the questions

- You believe that having a chance to answer the questions that I just asked would meet some of the needs we discussed earlier.

Encourage further conversation in the circle about how Lance and Pete might be feeling now after being asked these questions.

Section 7a: The RPM Getting Ready Process and Script

Suitable for RPMs who will be working with early years students

The way in which the RPMs will help students is guided by the 'RPM Getting Ready Process' (training manual – Early Years and Primary) and the 'RPM Script: Early Years and Primary' (see page 113). You may recognize this as a modified version of the *Early Years Restorative Conference Script* (Hansberry and Langley 2013).

This session takes the RPMs step by step through the *getting ready process* and the *script* that you just modelled to the group with the Lance and Pete scenario. We've included plenty of opportunities for conversation as the getting ready process and script is explained. This section of the training will take time. The RPMs will have many 'what if' questions, some of which we have considered below, based on our experience in training RPMs.

We have suggested some circle activities that work well to complement different parts of your teaching. However, you may find that the best approach is to have the RPMs sit in a circle, each with a copy of the *getting ready process* and the *script* to refer as you go through the process from start to finish, stopping regularly for paired or whole group conversation and questions.

This part of the training can be quite spontaneous. Groups often find themselves pausing for conversations, questions and even impromptu role plays to explore possible scenarios from different perspectives. Alternative ways to handle parts of the process may be suggested by the RPMs. This could even cause some changes to the *getting ready process* and *script* to better suit your own school(s)!

Materials needed

- 'RPM Getting Ready Process' projected on interactive whiteboard

- 'RPM Script' projected on interactive whiteboard

(Pdf versions are available at: www.jkp.com/catalogue/book/9781785923845 or www.hansberryec.com.au)

Getting Ready Step 1: Listen and paraphrase the student(s) reporting the problem:

1. Look at their face

2. Wait for a pause

3. Paraphrase the most important parts

4. Watch their face:

If they seem pleased or agree with you, move to Step 2.

If they look confused, grumpy, yell, cry, look upset or stop talking, say:

'You look upset, what else do you want to tell me?'

Take the reporting student to a place where you can properly hear them speak. Some students speak very quietly and others may have speech difficulties so they will be hard to understand in a noisy place.

This first part of the process is what we do when a student or a group comes to us with a problem. We use the skills of paraphrasing that we've already practised. When a student reports a problem to you, listening and paraphrasing will help you understand the problem and will make the student feel as though they are being listened to.

Below are questions that the RPMs may ask you about working with young people. If these are not asked, it's worth posing some of these questions to the RPMs to discuss in pairs, or in the circle:

• What if you can't understand the student?

• What it they are injured?

- What if they are crying and can't stop?

- What if they become upset while reporting the problem and start to cry

- What if the problem involves unsafe behaviour or a serious breaking of a school rule?

You may decide to record what the group agrees is a suitable response to the 'what if' scenarios.

Getting Ready Step 2: Say:

'That sounds tricky, thanks for telling me so calmly. Did you just want me to know or do you want some help?'

Wants some help:	**Just wanted you to know:**
⇩	*'What do you think you'll do to fix this?'*
'Okay, let's get the other(s) and have a chat about this.'	Listen to their idea, wish them luck and then watch how it goes.
	If able, check on how the student thinks it is going in five minutes.

This is an important part of the process because sometimes it's a little problem and the student just wants to tell somebody! We don't want to make a small problem bigger if we don't have to.

We also don't want to give young students the idea that someone bigger always has to fix their problems for them. This is bad for their resilience and problem solving skills.

Just wanted you to know:

'What do you think you'll do to fix this?'

Listen to their idea, wish them luck and then watch how it goes.

If able, check with the student how it is going in five minutes.

Questions for the RPMs

- How might they check in on that student later?

- What if it's a serious problem that you think you, or a teacher should get involved with?

- What if you think the student's idea to fix the problem will make the problem worse?

Wants some help:

'Okay, let's get the other(s) and have a chat about this.'

This is where we know that we are going to get involved with the problem and bring the students involved together for restorative mediation.

Getting Ready Step 3: Ask the student to go and ask the other students involved to come over for a chat OR walk with the student to where the other students are.

This stage of the process is very important.

Questions for the RPMs

- Is it best to send the reporting student to gather the others involved or should we walk over to the other students with the reporting student?

- What if you can't find the other students?

- What if the other students refuse to be part of mediation?

- What if the other students run away (what might be reasons they would run away?)

- What if the students become angry and or violent toward each other?

- What if the other student(s) begin to cry when you approach them?

Getting Ready Step 4: Take the students to a quieter place.

Questions for the RPMs

- Where might a quieter place be of you are on the oval, the playground, the quadrangle, the gym (have conversations specific to your school)?

- What if other students come, too? How do you ask them to leave?

Introduce yourselves

'Hi, I'm [name] and I'm an RPM. It's my job to help people sort problems out. [Name] came to me with a problem that they are worried about. They said you will be able to help us fix the problem. Will you help us? Great!'

Talking this way shows that you are friendly and helpful. It's also important to let students know that it's your job to help (a special responsibility given to you by the teachers), so you have some *authority*.

Show your RPM badge if you think it will help.

We introduce the problem to the student in a way that doesn't make it sound that they were *dobbed on* by the reporting student.

We say that the reporting student thought they'd be *a good person to help solve the problem*. This language is carefully chosen so nobody feels blamed. We then ask for their help, which again is important so nobody feels like they are the *bad guy*.

Some students will be very fearful of a bigger kid coming over to them and might worry that they are going to be teased or told off. Our face, body and voice send very important messages, so we need to think about how we might look to young children.

Pair share and feedback

» Why have we chosen these words to introduce ourselves?

» What feelings are we trying to trigger in the students?

» What feelings are we hoping we don't trigger?

» Because the students we work with are little, we only need to use a few words – can you think of another way you might introduce yourself?

'Who remembers the three rules for mediation?'

Be respectful, Be honest, Take turns to speak.

'Will you all follow these rules? That's great, this won't take long then.'

Whenever we have a 'restorative chat' in our school, we repeat these three rules that remind people how to keep the process fair.

We have to make these rules clear to young students and then we actually ask them if they will follow them. This is a respectful thing to do and also gets more commitment from the students involved.

1. To non-reporting student(s)

'[Reporting student] tells me that there's been a problem with ([explain problem briefly]. What happened?'

Paraphrase back to them what they said.

There's really no way of knowing who has made the *bad choices* until you've heard all of the students talk about the problem.

Because the reporting student has already told some of their story, it makes sense that the other students(s) get to tell their side at this part of the process.

Listen carefully because you may have already made judgements about what happened that are wrong. This is perfectly normal when we hear only one person's side of the problem and are trying to get a picture in our mind of what happened. It can be hard to change your mind and accept the new information because our brain doesn't like to change a story once it thinks it knows *what happened*. Just knowing this will help you be fairer.

Remember that your job isn't so much to decide whose fault the problem is; rather, it is to help the students explain the problem, listen to each other and see the problem from another person's viewpoint (which is often hard for little people).

We want to help the students think about *why they did what they did*, take some responsibility for their part of the problem and then come up with a way of fixing the problem.

They will be dealing with tricky feelings like fear, shame, anger, sadness and worry, just like we do when we have conflicts with friends.

Questions for the RPMs

» What if a school rule has been broken?

» What if somebody interrupts and disagrees with the way the story is being told?

» What if somebody starts yelling, points their finger or acts in a threatening way?

» How might we be able to tell if somebody is lying?

» What do we do if we think somebody might be lying?

2. To reporting student(s)

'What happened from your side?' (May be same or different.)

Paraphrase.

Even though you heard the reporting student's story when they first came to you, it may change once they hear the other student's story. This is normal and doesn't mean that anyone has lied. It just means that they have remembered more after hearing another account, or can now see the problem from the other person's point of view (which is good news).

If the story about the problem now matches, it's good news. If there are some differences, decide if they can be overlooked, or whether they are so important that you need to ask the students *if they are sure* about their side, or if they might have misunderstood something.

It's normal for young children to have understood events quite differently. The story of the *Six Blind Men and the Elephant* showed this. If important details of the problem can't be agreed on, you have some choices:

- Focus on the parts of their stories that they *do agree on* and don't spend any more time on the parts they've disagreed on and move to the next questions

- Sometimes, just summarizing the stories so far can help: *'We all agree on what happened up to the part where [insert details] but now we are stuck! [Name] believes that [insert details] happened and [name] believes that [insert details] happened! This doesn't mean that somebody is telling lies; it might just mean that we saw it differently. What should we do to get our story unstuck?'*

- If it comes to a point where the students are stuck and the process has come to a standstill, refer the students to a teacher or give them the option to stop the mediation at that point.

3. To students who made a bad choice (may be all of them)

'When you [describe what they did], was that:'

A good choice or a bad choice?

Or   The right thing or the wrong thing?

Or   Fair or unfair?

Or   Kind or unkind?' (Only use 1 or 2 of these.)

Paraphrase: 'So, you think it was...'

As you hear both sides of the problem, you will get a better idea of what has happened and how the actions of each of the students involved added to the problem.

This is where you will be able to ask questions to help the students think about what they did and to say whether these were good or bad choices.

This is the same as when we are asked *what we were thinking* when having a restorative chat with a teacher and other students. This question can be a little hard for young children, so we make it easier by asking these *closed questions*.

You can ask any of these questions; just choose the one that seems to fit the situation best. In the Lance and Pete scenario, I asked the 'fair or unfair' question.

If the student has trouble answering one of these questions, calmly ask them another one and give them time to answer.

Make sure you repeat their response so the other students hear it:

- 'So, you think doing [add details] was a bad choice?'

- 'So, you are saying that [add details] made the problem worse?'

- 'So, now you think that doing that was unfair?'

Then say something like, 'That's a very brave answer,' or, 'You're being very honest, that will help us fix this problem,' or, 'It takes lots of courage to say when you have done the wrong thing doesn't it?' This praises their honesty and often makes the others want to be just as honest and brave.

Questions for the RPMs

» What if they don't answer these questions?

» What if they give an answer opposite to what we are expecting?

» What if they don't answer and keep talking about what the others did that was wrong?

4. To students who were upset (may be all of them)

'How are you feeling about what's happened?'

'How do you think [name others] are feeling?'

Paraphrase:

> This is a very important part of the fixing because we are asking the students to say *how they are feeling* and they get to see that they are not the only ones feeling sad, angry, worried or scared about the problem.
>
> Little people often forget that other people have feelings as well, so this reminds them.
>
> The important part is to help them listen to each other when they say how they are feeling and then to say how the other person might be feeling.

Role play to demonstrate active listening

Because active listening is so important at this stage of the process, it's worth getting the RPMs to have a practice paraphrasing student's responses. The example below is a place to start, but have fun with making up different scenarios so that the RPMs can practise in groups of three.

RPM: 'Tom, how are you feeling about what happened?'

Tom: 'Sad.'

RPM (paraphrasing): 'So, you feel sad?'

Tom: 'Yeah.'

RPM: 'Tom, how do you think James might be feeling about what happened?'

Tom: 'Sad as well?'

RPM (paraphrasing): 'So, you think James might be feeling sad like you do?'

Tom: 'Yes.'

RPM: 'James, how are you feeling?'

James: 'Grumpy and Sad.'

RPM (paraphrasing): 'Grumpy and Sad?'

James: 'Yes, grumpy and sad.'

RPM: 'James, how is Tom feeling about what happened?'

James: 'He's sad.'

RPM: 'Wow! You two have done a great job of working out how each other is feeling! That's a very grown up thing to do!'

RPM: 'Tom and James, do you want to keep feeling sad and grumpy or should we try and fix this?'

5. To all students – beginning with the reporting student

'What can we do to fix this problem?'

Paraphrase:

You will hear all sorts of ideas when you ask the fixing question, some will be surprising!

Usually, young students will want to say sorry to each other and get on with playing together again without any hard feelings. Sometimes they want to give each other a hug, a hi-5 or just fix the problem by playing together again.

The great thing about little people is that they *don't usually* hold onto their hurts for long and forgive quickly.

Often, little people need some ideas about what they can do to fix the problem, especially if they haven't had much practice sorting out their own problems.

Sometimes, we might see that there's something obvious that could fix the problem like the students taking turns from now on, or agreeing on a fair way to share something.

Because you are older, with more experience, you will sometimes have good ideas that the little ones don't. In this case, it's okay to add your ideas. You might need to show them what you mean.

If there is anything else that needs fixing, you can add:

- 'I think you also need to [add your ideas]. Can you do this on your own or would you like some help?'

6. Checking on agreement

'So, to fix this problem you have agreed to [add details].' Ask each student, 'So, what is your part?'

'Thanks for letting me help you sort this out. Let's finish with a hi-5 or a handshake?'

This part is a final check on how well the students understand what they have agreed to do to fix the problem. It's very important to do this because little people can easily forget or misunderstand one another.

Record on the RPM report slip what has been agreed to fix the problem and then read it back to the students.

When you are happy that the students understand the plan, bring the mediation to a close.

Working with apologies

Sometimes, we need to teach children how to give and receive an apology. The words below can help:

Person apologising:

'[Name], I'm sorry for [describe behaviour].'

(Optional) 'I should have [new behaviour].'

Recipient:

'Thank you for your apology. I didn't like it when you [describe behaviour]. I felt [describe feelings].'

One important thing we can all teach younger students is how to make and receive an apology.

If an apology is part of the fixing for the students, you may help them with the words.

When a student says sorry, ask, 'What is it you are saying sorry for?' so they can describe the actions they regret. The student receiving an apology can be helped to say something other than, 'That's okay,' by thanking the other student for their apology and saying what it was they didn't like and how it felt.

Section 7b: The RPM Script

Suitable for RPMs who will be working with upper primary, middle and secondary students

The way the RPMs will help students is guided by the 'RPM Script: Middle & Secondary' (see pages 19 and 20).

This session takes the RPMs step by step through the *script* that you have just modelled to the group with the Lance and Pete scenario. We've included plenty of opportunities for conversation as the script is explained. This section of the training will take time. The RPMs will have many 'what if' questions, some of which we have added below from our experience in training RPMs.

We have suggested some circle activities that work well to complement different parts of your teaching. However, you may find that the best approach is to have the RPMs sit in a circle, each with a copy of the *script* to refer as you go through the process from start to finish, stopping regularly for paired or whole group conversation and questions.

This part of the training can be quite spontaneous. Groups often find themselves pausing for conversations, questions and even impromptu role plays to explore possible scenarios from different perspectives. Alternative ways to handle parts of the process may be suggested by the RPMs. This could even cause some changes to the *getting ready process* and *script* to better suit your own school(s)!

Materials needed

- 'RPM Getting Ready Process' projected on interactive whiteboard

- *'RPM Script: Middle & Secondary'* projected on interactive whiteboard

(PDF versions are available at: www.jkp.com/catalogue/book/9781785923845 or www.hansberryec.com.au)

Getting Ready Step 1: Listen and paraphrase the student(s) reporting the problem:

1. Look at their face

2. Wait for a pause

3. Paraphrase the most important parts

4. Watch their face:

If they seem pleased or agree with you, move to Step 2.

If they look confused, grumpy, yell, cry, look upset or stop talking, say:

'You look upset, what else do you want to tell me?'

Take the reporting student to a place where you can properly hear them speak. Some students speak very quietly and others may have speech difficulties so they will be hard to understand in a noisy place.

This first part of the process is what we do when a student or a group comes to us with a problem. We use the skills of paraphrasing that we've already practised. When a student reports a problem to you, listening and paraphrasing will help you understand the problem and will make the student feel as though they are being listened to.

Below are questions that the RPMs may ask you about working with young people. If these are not asked, it's worth posing some of these questions to the RPMs to discuss in pairs, or in the circle:

» What if you can't understand the student?

» What it they are injured?

» What if they are crying and can't stop?

» What if they become upset while reporting the problem and start to cry?

» What if the problem involves unsafe behaviour or a serious breaking of a school rule?

You may decide to record what the group agrees is a suitable response to the 'what if' scenarios.

Getting Ready Step 2: Say:

'That sounds tricky, thanks for telling me so calmly. Did you just want me to know or do you want some help?'

Wants some help:	Just wanted you to know:
⇩	*'What do you think you'll do to fix this?'*
'Okay, let's get the other(s) and have a chat about this.'	Listen to their idea, wish them luck and then watch how it goes.
	If able, check on how the student thinks it is going in five minutes.

This is an important part of the process because, sometimes, it's a little problem and the student just wants to tell somebody! We don't want to make a small problem bigger if we don't have to.

We also don't want to give young students the idea that someone bigger always has to fix their problems for them. This is bad for their resilience and problem solving skills.

Just wanted you to know:

'What do you think you'll do to fix this?'

Listen to their idea, wish them luck and then watch how it goes.

If able, check with the student how it is going in five minutes.

Questions for the RPMs:

How might they check in on that student later?

What if it's a serious problem that you think you, or a teacher should get involved with?

What if you think the student's idea to fix the problem will make the problem worse?

Wants some help:

'Okay, let's get the other(s) and have a chat about this.'

This is where we know that we are going to get involved with the problem and bring the students involved together for restorative mediation.

Getting Ready Step 3: Ask the student to go and ask the other students involved to come over for a chat OR walk with the student to where the other students are.

This stage of the process is very important.

Questions for the RPMs

- Is it best to send the reporting student to gather the others involved or should we walk over to the other students with the reporting student?

- What if you can't find the other students?

- What if the other students refuse to be part of mediation?

- What if the other students run away (what might be reasons they would run away)?

- What if the students become angry and or violent toward each other?

- What if the other student(s) begin to cry when you approach them?

Getting Ready Step 4: Take the students to a quieter place.

This first part of the process is what we do when a student or a group comes to us with a problem. We use the skills of paraphrasing that we've already practiced. When there's a conflict reported to you, listening and paraphrasing what the person says will help you understand the problem and will make those involved in the problem feel as though they are being listened to.

Questions for the RPMs

- Where might a quieter place be if you are on the oval, the playground, the quadrangle, the gym (have conversations specific to your school)?

- What if other students come too? How do you ask them to leave?

Introduce yourselves

'Hi, I'm [name] and I'm an RPM. It's my job to help people sort problems out. [Name] told me about a problem that they would like to sort out with you. They said they didn't want to make a big deal of it and didn't think teachers needed to be involved yet. Are you interested in solving the problem?'

Talking this way shows that you are there to help, not make the problem worse. It's also important to let students know that it's your job to help (a responsibility given to you by the teachers), so you have some *authority*. Being big-headed or cocky is never a good idea in this situation. Remain friendly and calm.

Show your RPM badge if you think it will help.

We introduce the problem to the student in a way that doesn't make it sound that they were *dobbed on* by the reporting student.

We say that the reporting student wants the problem kept small (they don't want to anyone to get into trouble). This language is carefully chosen so nobody feels blamed. We then ask for their help, which again is important so nobody feels like they are being blamed.

Some students will be very defensive or suspicious of you. Some may treat it as a big joke! This is normal. Stay calm and friendly and, if necessary, calmly repeat that you are a peer mediator and it is your job to help keep problems small. Your face, body and voice send very important messages so we need to think about how we might look to others.

Pair share and feedback

» Why have we chosen these words to introduce ourselves?

» What emotions are we trying to trigger in the students?

» What emotions are we hoping we don't trigger?

» Can you think of another way you might introduce yourself that is respectful and firm at the same time?

'There are three rules of engagement when sorting conflicts, they are:

Be respectful, Be honest, Take turns to speak.

Can you all follow these? Okay, this won't take long then.'

Whenever we have a 'restorative chat' in our school, regardless of what aged students we are working with, we repeat these rules of engagement to remind people how to keep the process fair.

We have to make these rules of engagement clear and we actually ask for a commitment from the other students to follow them. With older students, setting out the rules of engagement may feel strange, but it has to be done so people know what to expect from one another.

1. To non-reporting student(s)

'[Reporting student] tells me that there's been a problem with [explain problem briefly]. What happened?'

Paraphrase back to them what they said.

There's really no way of knowing who has made the *bad choices* until you've heard all of the students talk about the problem.

Because the reporting student has already told you their version of events, it makes sense that the other students(s) get to tell their version at this point in the process.

Listen carefully because you may have already made judgements about what happened that are wrong. This is perfectly normal when we hear only one person's side of the problem and are trying to get a picture in our mind of what happened. It can be hard to change your mind and accept the new information because our brain doesn't like to change a story once it thinks it knows *what happened.* Just knowing this will help you be more balanced.

Remember that your job isn't so much to decide whose fault the problem is; rather, it is to help the students explain the problem, listen to each other and see the problem from another person's viewpoint (which is much easier for some students than it is for others).

We want to help those involved think about *why they did what they did,* take some responsibility for their part of the problem and then come up with a way of fixing the problem.

They will be dealing with tricky feelings like fear, shame, anger, sadness and worry, just like we do when we have conflicts with others.

Questions for the RPMs

» What if there has been a serious breaking of a school rule in the reported problem?

» What if somebody interrupts and disagrees with the way the story is being told?

» What if somebody starts yelling, points their finger or acts in a threatening way?

» What kinds of conditions make it hard for some people to see a problem from another's viewpoint?[4]

» What can help in these situations?

» What do we do if it appears that someone isn't interested in solving the problem and is making a mockery of the process?

» What do we do if we think somebody might be lying?

---

4   *Restorative Practices and Special Needs* (Burnett and Thorsborne 2015) provides a useful exploration of using RPs with students with conditions that fall under the special needs umbrella. Parts of this resource may be useful in this training for older students to help them understand some of the social and communication difficulties some students encounter when working through conflict.

2. To reporting student(s)

'What happened from your side?' (May be same or different.)

Paraphrase.

Even though you heard the reporting student's story when they first came to you, it may change once they hear the other student's story. This is normal and doesn't mean that anyone has lied. It just means that they have remembered more after hearing another account, or can now see the problem from the other person's point of view (which is good news).

If the story about the problem now matches (or almost matches), it's good news. If there are some differences (which happens most of the time), decide if they can be overlooked. You might say, 'We just can't agree on this part of the story. Does this have to hold us up or can be keep going?'

It's normal for people to have understood events quite differently. The story of *Six Blind Men and the Elephant* showed this. If important details of the problem can't be agreed on, you have some choices:

- Focus on the parts of their stories that they *do agree on* and don't spend any more time on the parts they've disagreed on and move to the next questions

- Sometimes just summarising the stories so far can help: *'We all agree on what happened up to the part where [add details but now we are stuck! [Name] believes that [add details] happened and [name] believes that [add details] happened! This doesn't mean that somebody is telling lies; it might just mean that we saw it differently. What should we do about this?'*

- If it comes to a point where the students are stuck and the process has come to a standstill, refer the students to a teacher or give them the option to stop the mediation at that point.

3. To students who made a bad choice (may be all of them)

'What were you hoping would happen when you [say what they did]?' OR 'What made you decide to do/say that?'

You may decide to go a step further and ask these closed questions to help:

Was that a good choice or a bad choice?

Or   Was that a good look or a bad look?

Or   Was that fair or unfair?

Or   Did that make the problem better or worse for you all?

Paraphrase: 'So, you think it was...'

As you hear both sides of the problem, you will get a better idea of what has happened and how the actions of each of the students involved added to the problem.

This is where you will be able to ask questions to help the students think about what they did and to say whether these were good or bad choices.

You can ask any of these listed questions; just choose the one that seems to fit the situation best. In the Lance and Pete scenario, I asked the 'fair or unfair' question.

If a student has trouble answering one of these questions, you might calmly ask them another one and give them time to answer.

Make sure you repeat their response so the other students hear it:

- 'So, you think doing [add details] was a bad choice?'

- 'So, you are saying that [add details] made the problem worse?'

- 'So, now you think that doing that was unfair?'

Then thank them for their responses.

Questions for the RPMs

» What if they don't answer these questions?

» What if they give an answer opposite to what we are expecting?

» What if they don't answer and keep talking about what the others did that was wrong?

» What if someone becomes disrespectful?

4. To students who were upset (may be all of them)

'How has this affected you?'

'Who else has been affected?'

'How do you think this has affected others?'

Paraphrase.

> This is a very important part of the process because we are asking the students to say *how they have been affected* and they get to see that they are not the only ones affected by the problem.
>
> The important part is to help them listen to each other when they say how they've been affected then to hear how the other person has been affected.
>
> Expect that students may not use the term 'affected', instead, using terms like 'annoyed' or even 'pissed off'!

Role play to demonstrate active listening

Because active listening is so important at this stage of the process, it's worth getting the RPMs to have a practice paraphrasing student's responses. The example below is a place to start, but have fun with making up different scenarios so the RPMs can practise in groups of three:

RPM: 'Lance, how has this affected you?'

Lance: 'I dunno, I was really annoyed when Pete brought my mum into it the way he did just because he lost a game of around the world. He made it really personal.'

RPM (paraphrasing): 'Pete's comment crossed the line.'

Lance: 'Yeah.'

RPM: 'Lance, who else do you think has been affected?'

Lance: 'John?'

RPM: 'How do you think John might have been affected?'

Lance: 'He's probably over the comments about people's families as well.'

RPM: 'So, you think he's over it like you are?'

Lance: 'Probably.'

RPM: 'John, how have you been affected by this?'

John: 'It's really made things sour.'

RPM: 'So, it's changed things between you three?'

John: 'Yeah.'

5. To all students – usually beginning with the reporting student

'What can we do to fix this problem?' OR *'Do you want to keep the conflict going or should we try to work it out?'*

Paraphrase.

You will hear all sorts of ideas when you ask the sorting-out question, some will be surprising!

Sometimes, people involved will want to just get on with their lives with an agreement to stop the conflict and will consider the problem fixed just because they've agreed that the conflict has been annoying for all involved.

Sometimes, people might need some suggestions from the RPM about how the problem might be fixed, especially if they haven't had much experience sorting out their own problems.

Sometimes, we might see that there's something obvious that could fix the problem like the students taking turns from now on, or agreeing on a fair way to share an area.

It's okay to add your ideas. You might need to show them what you mean.

6. Checking on agreement

'So, to sort this out, you have agreed to [add details].' Ask each student: *'So, what is your part?'*

'Is there anything anyone wants to add, or say to the other before we finish?'

'Thanks for letting me help you sort this out.'

This part is a final check how well the students understand what they have agreed to do to fix the problem. It's very important to do this because people can easily misunderstand one another.

Record on the RPM report slip what has been agreed to fix the problem and then read it back to the students.

When you are happy that the students understand the plan, bring the mediation to a close.

Working with apologies

Don't expect that apologies will be made and certainly don't try to force anyone to make an apology. If they happen naturally, great. If not, remember that often it's enough for people to know that the other people in the conflict understand that what they did wrong and that both sides want the problem sorted out. Trying to squeeze apologies out of people can cause more problems than it is worth and can even cause the process to go backward.

Apologies sometimes happen when we ask the last question: *'Is there anything anyone wants to add, or say to the other before we finish?'* If an apology is made, you might ask:

'Can you tell us what you are apologizing for?'

You may also ask the person who received the apology:

'How are you with that?'

Notice that we are not asking, *'Do you accept that apology?'* This is a loaded question and can make people feel as though they have to accept an apology when all we really want them to do is acknowledge that they have been apologized to.

★

Section 8: Time to practise!

Now that the RPMs have seen the RPM process role played by you and have been through the process together, it's time for them to have a go themselves. For this, RPMs will be randomly placed into groups of three and will each have turns playing students and RPMs for about an hour. During this practice time, we want to help the RPMs stay as on task as possible so they all get plenty of opportunities to use the process. This means that you will need to engage closely with the groups as you move around the groups. A large space (like an open space area of gymnasium) also works best so that the RPMs can spread out and hear themselves talk (and think) as they role play.

Okay RPMs. You've learned so much today that it's time now to have a go at using the process with each other before we let you loose on other students!

This means that you will take turns playing the roles of RPM and of students who are having a problem.

It also means that we will have to have some scenarios, like the Lance and Pete scenario to practice with.

Silent statements

To start, we'll get ourselves up and moving again. Find your RPM training manual and have it in your hand.

Silently change places if:

- You are wearing any form of jewellery

- You're looking forward to starting to work as an RPM

- You're a bit worried about not remembering the RPM process that we just looked at.

So, I can see that lots of us are feeling the same way about wanting to do well as RPMs. That's totally normal. If you weren't a little nervous I'd be worried!

Check that the circle is mixed up and then count off threes around the circle to put RPMs into teams of three.

> Now that we are in teams of three, we had better make some agreements about how the role plays will work so that we can all get the most out of them.
>
> We will keep it simple and have two students who are having a problem and one RPM. You will switch jobs so that everyone gets a few turns at being an RPM.
>
> Now we need some ideas for scenarios. Can everybody open their training manual to where we listed some of the types of conflicts that happen on the yard that RPMs would be able to help students with?

Set the groups the task of practising the process with the different scenarios. Encourage groups to try each other's scenarios. Encourage RPMs to use their process cards.

After an hour, bring practice to an end.

Section 9: Concluding Circle

Bring the RPMs back into a circle and make sure that they have their training manuals and other belongings with them.

> Well, RPMs, this brings the phase 1 training to an end.
>
> Your brains would be just about ready to explode. We have talked about so much today and learned some new skills. Don't expect to be excellent at these skills straight away. Becoming a good RPM will take practice and mistakes.
>
> To finish, think of one word that describes how you feel after today's training and be ready to share in a go-around. Remember, you can pass!

3A RPM PHASE 1 TRAINING MANUAL

Suitable for RPMs Working with Early Years and Primary-Aged Students

Warm-up: People Bingo (Resource 1)

Can play a musical instrument	Has been in a plane	Has the same size hand as you
Has been camping	Gets out of bed the same time as you	Has the same number of siblings as you
Likes a musical artist you like	Enjoys bike riding	Walks to school
Has a dog as a pet	Barracks for a football team	Has seen a movie at a cinema in the last month
Has been attended a live sports game this year	Has blue eyes	Favourite colour is green

Restorative Peer Mediation (RPM) – What is it?

Our definition of an RPM

My definition of an RPM

Conflicts that occur in our schoolyard

Remember that most conflicts that occur in the yard are appropriate for RPMs, but some are better handled by a teacher.

Topic 1: Paraphrasing

Paraphrasing is a skill that is very important for RPMs. When we paraphrase well, the person talking will feel as though we are listening and understanding what they are saying. This is important so they can tell us what has happened and we can understand properly.

There is a recipe for good paraphrasing:

1. Look and listen to the person talking – look at their face

2. Wait for a pause in what they are saying and

3. Say back in just a few words the most important parts of what they have just said:

   » *So you felt...*

   » *They were...*

   » *It was...*

   » *You were...*

You know you are paraphrasing well when the other person:

- Looks up at you for a second after you paraphrase

- Keeps talking with even more enthusiasm after you have paraphrased

- Nods, smiles, or does something else to show that they like what you said.

You might be doing too much paraphrasing when the other person:

- Stops and goes quiet

- Shakes their head

- Looks angry or irritated after you paraphrase

- Says something like, 'Don't interrupt me'!

You will discover that:

- Trying to paraphrase too much sounds like interrupting and is frustrating for the person talking.

- Making your paraphrases too long makes it seem as though you have taken over and this will stop the other person talking

- You should never begin telling your own story when you're supposed to be the one listening.

Topic 2: Understanding people's needs when they are hurt, or have hurt others

THE SOCCER STORY

Pete, John and Lance were playing with a soccer ball at recess time. They were taking turns to try to kick the ball into the goals. It was Pete's turn. John and Lance stood in front of goals as the two goal keepers – it was their job to try to stop the ball going through when Pete kicked it. Pete was the only one who hadn't scored a goal. John and Lance had kicked a goal each. Pete was worried that he'd be the only one who hadn't kicked a goal. He didn't want to look like a bad soccer player.

Pete took a big run-up and kicked as hard as he could. The ball went flying through the air toward the goals – it was a great kick and looked as though it would be a goal for sure. Lance knew he'd have to jump as high as he could to stop the goal. He shut his eyes and jumped with his arms outstretched as high as he could. The ball just touched the tips of his fingers and then flew over the top of the goals. Lance and his tremendous leap had just stopped a certain goal!

When Pete saw that Lance had stopped the goal, his face turned to thunder. He thought to himself, 'The bell is going and I'm the only one who hasn't scored a goal.' He felt his stomach tighten into a knot and his face get really hot. His feelings were taking control of him. Pete picked up the soccer ball and yelled at Lance, 'You're a stupid cheat; you're not playing with us at lunch time.' John yelled angrily at Pete, 'That's not fair! You can't play with us at lunch!'

What do we need when we are hurt or when we hurt others?

Can you see any similarities between these two lists? What are they?

When we are hurt,
we need...

When we hurt others,
we need...

People usually need the same kinds of things to feel better when they've been hurt by the words or actions of others.

Topic 3: Seeing things differently

Most young children think that others see the world just as they do and think what they think. This means they they have trouble understanding that someone might see an event or problem differently to how they saw it. This is called being *egocentric* and it is part of being little. We all grow out of it as our brain develops.

To be an RPM, we need to understand that children will often see events differently, depending on their viewpoint – where they were sitting or standing when the problem happened, what they heard (or didn't hear) and even what they *were expecting* to happen.

There will be times when you are listening to children's stories about *what happened* when children will think that another child is lying because their version of what happened is different to theirs. Because they are still learning that we can *see things differently*, they may accuse each other of telling lies.

Sometimes, someone will be lying, but not as often as you might think.

We need to help younger children understand that when people tell a different story about *what happened,* it doesn't automatically mean that the other person is telling lies and being dishonest. It can often be that the other person was watching from a different place, or may have seen or heard different things to them.

The story of the *Six Blind Men and the Elephant* is a great story to illustrate how we can all think different things about the same thing. In other words, we can *perceive* things differently.

THE SIX BLIND MEN AND THE ELEPHANT

Once upon a time, there lived six blind men in a village. Being blind meant that their eyes didn't work properly and they couldn't see. One day the villagers told them, 'Hey, there is an elephant in the village today.'

The six blind men had no idea what an elephant was. They decided, 'Even though we will not be able to see it, let's go and feel it anyway.' All of them went to where the elephant was. Each of them touched the elephant.

'Hey, the elephant is like a pillar that holds a large building up,' said the first man, who touched the elephant's leg.

'No! It is like a rope,' said the second man, who touched the tail.

'No! It is like a thick branch of a tree,' said the third man, who touched the trunk of the elephant.

'It is like a big hand fan,' said the fourth man, who touched the ear of the elephant.

'It is like a huge wall,' said the fifth man, who touched the side of the elephant.

'It is like a solid pipe,' said the sixth man, who touched the tusk of the elephant.

They began to argue about the elephant and every one of them insisted that he was right. The six men were getting angry with one another.

A wise man was passing by and he saw this. He stopped and asked them, 'What is the matter?' They said, 'We cannot agree on what the elephant is like.' Each one of them said what he thought the elephant was like. The wise man calmly explained to them, 'All of you are right. The reason every one of you is telling it differently because you all felt a different part of the elephant. So, the elephant is like all of the things you said.'

'Oh!' the six blind men said. There was no more fighting. The six blind men felt happy that they were all right.

The moral of the story is that there may be some truth to what someone says, even if their story is different to ours. So, instead of arguing like the blind men, we can say, 'Maybe you saw it differently to me.' This way we don't get in as many arguments.

RPM Getting Ready Process

Getting Ready Step 1: Listen and paraphrase the student(s) reporting the problem:

1. Look at their face

2. Wait for a pause

3. Paraphrase the most important parts

4. Watch their face:

If they seem pleased or agree with you, move to Step 2.

If they look confused, grumpy, yell, cry, look upset or stop talking, say:

'You look upset, what else do you want to tell me?'

Getting Ready Step 2: Say:

'That sounds tricky, thanks for telling me so calmly. Did you just want me to know or do you want some help?'

Wants some help:	Just wanted you to know:
⇩	*'What do you think you'll do to fix this?'*
'Okay, let's get the other(s) and have a chat about this.'	Listen to their idea, wish them luck and then watch how it goes.
	If able, check on how the student thinks it is going in five minutes.

Getting Ready Step 3: Ask the student to go and ask the other students involved to come over for a chat OR walk with the student to where the other students are.

This stage of the process is very important.

Getting Ready Step 4: Take the students to a quieter place.

RPM Script: Early Years and Primary

Introduce yourselves:

'Hi, I'm [name] and I'm an RPM. It's my job to help people sort out problems. [Name] came to me with a problem that they are worried about. They said you will be able to help us fix the problem. Will you help us? Great!'

'Who remembers the three rules for mediation?'

Be respectful, Be honest, Take turns to speak.

'Will you all follow these rules? That's great, this won't take long then.'

1. To non-reporting student(s):

'[Reporting student] tells me that there's been a problem with [explain problem briefly]. What happened?'

Paraphrase back to them what they said.

2. To reporting student(s):

'What happened from your side?' (May be same or different.)

Paraphrase.

3. To students who made a bad choice (may be all of them):

'When you [describe what they did] was that:

> A good choice or a bad choice?

Or   The right thing or the wrong thing?

Or   Fair or unfair?

Or   Kind or unkind?' *(Only use 1 or 2 of these.)*

Paraphrase: 'So, you think it was...'

4. To students who were upset (may be all of them):

'How are you feeling about what's happened?'

'How do you think [name others] are feeling?'

Paraphrase.

5. To all students – beginning with the reporting student:

'What can we do to fix this problem?'

Paraphrase.

If there is anything else that needs fixing, you can add:

> » *'I think you also need to [add details].'*

> » *'Can you do this on your own or would you like some help?'*

6. Checking on agreement:

'So, to fix this problem, you have agreed to [add details].' Ask each student, 'So, what is your part?'

'Thanks for letting me help you sort this out. Let's finish with a hi-5 or a handshake?'

Complete the RPM report and place it into the RPM folder.

3B RPM PHASE 1 TRAINING MANUAL

Suitable for RPMs Working with Middle School and Secondary-Aged Students

Warm-up: People Bingo

Can play a musical instrument	Has been in a plane	Has the same size hand as you
Has been camping	Gets out of bed the same time as you	Has the same number of siblings as you
Likes a musical artist you like	Enjoys bike riding	Walks to school
Has a dog as a pet	Barracks for a football team	Has seen a movie at a cinema in the last month
Has been attended a live sports game this year	Has blue eyes	Favourite colour is green

Restorative Peer Mediation (RPM) – What is it?

Our definition of an RPM

My definition of an RPM

Conflicts that occur in our schoolyard

Remember that most conflicts that occur in the yard are appropriate for RPMs, but some are better handled by a teacher.

Topic 1: Paraphrasing

Paraphrasing is a skill that is very important for RPMs. When we paraphrase well, the person talking will feel as though we are listening and understanding what they are saying. This is important so they can tell us what has happened and we can understand properly.

There is a recipe for good paraphrasing:

1. Look and listen to the person talking – look at their face

2. Wait for a pause in what they are saying and

3. Say back in just a few words the most important parts of what they have just said:

   » *So you felt...*

   » *They were...*

   » *It was...*

   » *You were...*

You know you are paraphrasing well when the other person:

- Looks up at you for a second after you paraphrase

- Keeps talking with even more enthusiasm after you have paraphrased

- Nods, smiles or does something else to show that they like what you said.

You might be doing too much paraphrasing when the other person:

- Stops and goes quiet

- Shakes their head

- Looks angry or irritated after you paraphrase

- Says something like, 'Don't interrupt me!'

You will discover that:

- Trying to paraphrase too much sounds like interrupting and is frustrating for the person talking

- Making your paraphrases too long makes it seem as though you have taken over and this will stop the other person talking

- You should never begin telling your own story when you're supposed to be the one listening.

Topic 2: Understanding people's needs when they are hurt, or have hurt others

THE SOCCER STORY

Pete, John and Lance were playing with a soccer ball at recess time. They were taking turns to try to kick the ball into the goals. It was Pete's turn. John and Lance stood in front of goals as the two goal keepers – it was their job to try to stop the ball going through when Pete kicked it. Pete was the only one who hadn't scored a goal. John and Lance had kicked a goal each. Pete was worried that he'd be the only one who hadn't kicked a goal. He didn't want to look like a bad soccer player.

Pete took a big run-up and kicked as hard as he could. The ball went flying through the air toward the goals – it was a great kick and looked as though it would be a goal for sure. Lance knew he'd have to jump as high as he could to stop the goal. He shut his eyes and jumped with his arms outstretched as high as he could. The ball just touched the tips of his fingers and then flew over the top of the goals. Lance and his tremendous leap had just stopped a certain goal!

When Pete saw that Lance had stopped the goal, his face turned to thunder. He thought to himself, 'The bell is going and I'm the only one who hasn't scored a goal.' He felt his stomach tighten into a knot and his face get really hot. His feelings were taking control of him. Pete picked up the soccer ball and yelled at Lance, 'You're a stupid cheat; you're not playing with us at lunch time.' John yelled angrily at Pete, 'That's not fair! You can't play with us at lunch!'

THE BASKETBALL STORY

Now, imagine that Lance, Pete and John weren't little kids, they are now 13-year-olds playing a game of around the world at the basketball courts.

John, Lance and Pete were playing a game of around the world on the basketball courts. It was a game where the winner was the first to sink a shot from different places on the court and finally a long shot. If a person scored, they moved to the next place for a bonus shot. If they missed, it was the next person's go. The winner finished first.

John had already shot and scored from all places so it was down to Lance and Pete. They were both on the long shot spot and the first to sink it would come in 2nd place. Pete had come last in the last two games and was starting to feel pretty uptight about the prospect of coming last again. There'd been some friendly trash talk between the boys and Pete was getting edgy as Lance got ready to shoot his pong shot. If Lance hit the shot, Pete was going to be last...again.

Lance looked at Pete, winked at him and said, 'Game over, bitch.' He shot the ball. It looked perfectly straight out of his hand. It sailed through the air on the perfect arc and then, swish! Nothing but net.

Lance turned to Pete and shouted, 'Yeah!' as he pumped his fist in the air close to Pete's face. Pete felt a wave of anger wash over him. His jaw clenched and his shoulders pulled back. Pete eyeballed Lance and said, 'You shoot well for a guy with a retard for a mum.'

This was a bad enough thing to say to someone but what made it worse was that Lance's mother had recently been diagnosed with Multiple Sclerosis. Pete knew this and, in his embarrassment about coming last, he made an insult of it. He had crossed the line. This wasn't banter; it was one of the worst things you could say to someone.

Lance couldn't believe what Pete had just said. He froze to the spot, wide eyed. His mouth hung open. After a moment, John said to Pete, 'Dude, that was unnecessary.' Pete felt sick about his cruel and jealous comment but instead of admitting he was wrong, he said, 'That's what you get if you get up in my face.' John just shook his head. Pete knew he had crossed a line that should never be crossed. Insulting someone's mum was bad enough, but to make an insult about a serious illness was unspeakable. He wished he could take it back. Lance was fighting back tears. He was so ashamed, even though he was the victim of Pete's comment.

Lance wanted to run at Pete and knock him down to defend his mum's honour, but he knew Pete was stronger than him. He took a deep breath and then said to Pete, 'I'm getting an RPM before I decide to cave your head in.'

What do we need when we are hurt or when we hurt others?

Can you see any similarities between these two lists? What are they?

When we are hurt,
we need...

When we hurt others,
we need...

People usually need the same kinds of things to feel better when they've been hurt by the words or actions of others.

Topic 3: Seeing things differently

The ability to see a situation or an event from another person's perspective varies from person to person. Some people are very good at it and some people need lots of help to do this and believe that the only way to interpret an event is the way they interpret it. They can believe that everyone else is lying and they are the only ones telling the truth. We all get stuck in our own perspective from time to time but for some people this is an ongoing problem. These tend to be the people who find themselves in conflict more often than others.

To be an RPM we need to understand that people in conflict will often see events differently, depending on their viewpoint – where they were sitting or standing when the problem happened, what they heard (or didn't hear) and even what they *were expecting* to happen.

There will be times when you are listening to someone's version of events about *what happened* when they will insist that another person is lying because that person's version of what happened is different to theirs.

There will be times when someone will be intentionally lying, but not as often as you might think.

Part of mediation is helping people understand that when people tell a different story about *what happened*, it doesn't automatically mean that the other person is telling lies and being dishonest. It can often be that the other person was watching from a different place, or may have seen or heard different things to them.

The fable of the *Six Blind Men and the Elephant* is a great story to illustrate how we can all think different things about the same thing. In other words, we can *perceive* things differently.

THE SIX BLIND MEN AND THE ELEPHANT

Once upon a time, there lived six blind men in a village. Being blind meant that their eyes didn't work properly and they couldn't see. One day, the villagers told them, 'Hey, there is an elephant in the village today.'

The six blind men had no idea what an elephant was. They decided, 'Even though we will not be able to see it, let's go and feel it anyway.' All of them went to where the elephant was. Each of them touched the elephant.

'Hey, the elephant is like a pillar that holds a large building up,' said the first man, who touched the elephant's leg.

'No! It is like a rope,' said the second man, who touched the tail.

'No! It is like a thick branch of a tree,' said the third man, who touched the trunk of the elephant.

'It is like a big hand fan,' said the fourth man, who touched the ear of the elephant.

'It is like a huge wall,' said the fifth man, who touched the side of the elephant.

'It is like a solid pipe,' said the sixth man, who touched the tusk of the elephant.

They began to argue about the elephant and every one of them insisted that he was right. The six men were getting angry with one another.

A wise man was passing by and he saw this. He stopped and asked them, 'What is the matter?' They said, 'We cannot agree on what the elephant is like.' Each one of them said what he thought the elephant was like. The wise man calmly explained to them, 'All of you are right. The reason every one of you is telling it differently because you all felt a different part of the elephant. So, the elephant is like all of the things you said.'

'Oh!' the six blind men said. There was no more fighting. The six blind men felt happy that they were all right.

The moral of the story is that there may be some truth to what someone says, even if their story is different to ours. So, instead of arguing like the blind men, we can say, 'Maybe you saw it differently to me.' This way we don't get in as many arguments.

RPM Script: Middle & Secondary

Introduce yourselves

'Hi, I'm [name] and I'm an RPM. It's my job to help people sort out problems. [Name] told me about a problem that they would like to sort out with you. They said they didn't want to make a big deal of it and didn't think teachers needed to be involved yet. Are you interested in solving the problem?'

'There are three rules of engagement when sorting conflicts, they are:

Be respectful, Be honest, Take turns to speak.

Can you all follow these rules? Okay, this won't take long then.'

1. To non-reporting student(s)

'[Reporting student] tells me that there's been a problem with [explain problem briefly]. What happened?'

Paraphrase back to them what they said.

2. To reporting student(s)

'What happened from your side?' (May be same or different.)

Paraphrase.

3. To students who made a bad choice (may be all of them)

'What were you hoping would happen when you [say what they did]?' OR 'What made you decide to do/say that?'

You may decide to go a step further and ask these closed questions to help:

> Was that a good choice or a bad choice?

Or   Was that a good look or a bad look?

Or   Was that fair or unfair?

Or   Did that make the problem better or worse for you all?

Paraphrase: 'So, you think it was...'

Choose the most appropriate question; you may need to ask more than one of these questions for the student to understand what you are asking.

4. To students who were upset (may be all of them)

'How has this affected you?'

'Who else has been affected?'

'How do you think this has affected others?'

Paraphrase.

5. To all students – usually beginning with the reporting student

'What can we do to fix this problem?' OR 'Do you want to keep the conflict going or should we try to work it out?'

Paraphrase.

6. Checking on agreement

'So, to sort this out you have agreed to [add details].' Ask each student: 'So, what is your part?'

'Is there anything anyone wants to add, or say to the other before we finish?'

'Thanks for letting me help you sort this out.'

Complete the RPM report and place it into the RPM folder.

4

GETTING STARTED

After phase 1 training

Following the phase 1 training day there will be work to do to get the RPMs on the beat and using the skills they have learned in training. Below are tasks and tips that experience has shown us that get your RPMs off to a good start.

Creating the duty roster

RPMs work in pairs, so they will need to be paired up with *duty buddies*. These teams will ideally go 'on duty' as RPMs together, one break time per week. At the end of the phase 1 training, ask the RPMs to talk with their teachers and parents and create you a list of times that they *cannot* be on duty during the week. Only begin pairing RPMs and creating the RPM duty roster once you know the availability of RPMs.

Introductions

Organizing for the RPMs to be introduced to the school community is an important step in making everyone aware of who the RPMs are and what their role will be in the yard. It is ideal to get the RPMs to introduce themselves, initially at a whole school assembly and visiting homerooms/classrooms soon after for a more personal meet and greet. A suggested script for RPMs to use for classroom visits is on page 127 of the Introduction.

RPM folders

Folders for the RPMs to use while on duty need to be organized and ready to go after the phase 1 training. These folders should contain:

- Rules for Mediation (Appendix 2)

- A laminated RPM Script for the appropriate age group (Appendices 3 and 4)

- RPM reporting sheets (Appendix 5) copied and ready to go.

- A pen attached to the folders.

Other considerations

It is important for the RPMs to know what the process is for when they are 'on duty'. Some things to consider include:

- Where the different duty areas are

- Where the RPM folders will be stored

- Where completed reporting sheets will go

- Where refill reporting sheets are stored

- What to do if students or incidents need to be followed up by RPMs or teachers.

All of these processes and procedures are best sorted out before the RPMs begin their important work with students in the yard. Because of this, we recommend a follow-up meeting in the days after the initial phase 1 training.

Despite the best planning, there will always be other issues that come to light only after RPMs have started their work. Phase 2 training will be the ideal forum to address these.

The next section of this manual gives helpful guidance for creating a school policy document for RPM that will fit alongside existing whole school wellbeing policies.

5

PUTTING THE RPM PROGRAM INTO SCHOOL POLICY

It is important to embed the RPM program within the school's policies in *restorative practices*, *wellbeing* and any other policy relevant to *developing social and emotional competencies*, *student voice*, *student agency* or *school safety*. This sends the message that the RPM program is valued and is here to stay.

Below is an example of what might go into your school's policies on the RPM program.

Restorative Peer Mediation at Restorative Town School

At our school, we value a culture of working restoratively and cooperatively. We skill our students to solve conflicts peacefully and safely. Our Restorative Peer Mediation (RPM) program fits within this philosophy. Trained Restorative Peer Mediators (RPMs) work alongside duty teachers to create a safe atmosphere in the schoolyard by assisting students who find themselves in conflict to find solutions that are agreed to by all involved. As with all restorative practices in our school, the goal is to empower students to take responsibility for their actions and to problem solve constructively. Peer mediation programs have been proven to positively affect school climate and student conduct:

> A well-conducted peer mediation program can be successful in changing the way students approach conflict... The use of peer mediation can substantially change how students approach and settle conflicts... These changes in turn appear to lead to...positive outcomes. Student attitudes toward negotiation may become more positive, with students expressing a greater willingness to help friends avoid fights and solve problems and less likely to believe that certain individuals deserve to be 'beaten up'. ...a number of [studies] have reported that both students and teachers believe that peer mediation significantly improved their school climate. There is also evidence that implementing peer mediation programs can be associated with fewer fights, fewer referrals to the office, and a decreased rate of school suspension. Finally, for the student meditors themselves,

learning the mediation process has been shown to increase self-esteem and even improve academic achievement. (Skiba and Peterson 2003, pp.1–2)

Aims of the RPM program

- To build a more peaceful and safer school

- To promote a restorative culture in our school

- To increase trust in our senior students from younger students

- To develop a sense of *agency* and *service to others* in our senior students

- To develop and allow an outlet for nurturing qualities in our senior students

- To build RPMs' awareness of conflict and non-violent ways to respond to it

- To develop an understanding of conflict and how it can be used to promote learning and resilience

- To develop interpersonal skills such as active listening, paraphrasing and win-win problem solving that the RPMs can use in in their own lives as well as when working as an RPM

- To develop restorative problem solving skills in both RPMs and other students

- To increase the school's capacity to respond to student conflict in restorative ways.

Organization

Our school's Restorative Peer Mediation coordinator will run the program. Their role is to:

- Run the selection process for RPMs at the beginning of each school year

- Conduct phase 1 training for RPMs

- promote the RPM program within the school community

- Schedule and coordinate ongoing fortnightly phase 2 training meetings where RPMs debrief, share experiences, review difficult situations and receive additional training

- Manage the RPM roster

- Liaise between RPMs and teaching staff

- Follow up (when necessary) with students involved in the conflicts that have been mediated by RPMs.

Peer mediation selection and training

Peer Mediators are selected by the RPM coordinator and other relevant staff (particularly class teachers of potential RPMs). Values and skills we seek in RPMs include trustworthiness, helpfulness and respect for individual differences. A cross-section of students representing the ethnicity, socioeconomic level and gender of the school population are selected for the program.

Parent cooperation is necessary for the success of the program. A letter will be sent informing parents/caregivers of their child's role and responsibilities as an RPM; this will include a permission form for the parent/caregiver to sign.

Phase 1 and 2 training will:

- Define Peer Mediation and causes of conflict in schools

- Teach qualities and skills of a Peer Mediator – listening skills, questioning, problem solving and using restorative questions

- Give participants the opportunity to use and practice the mediation script through role play

- Allow time for discussion of and setting up of the Peer Mediation program in the school

- Continually develop RPMs' skills.

The process of implementation

1. Senior students are introduced to the role and responsibilities of RPMs and invited apply to be an RPM.

2. Applications are read and a group of students is selected to be a part of the program by the RPM coordinator in collaboration with relevant staff.

3. Parents are informed of their child's intent to participate in the program via a letter with a return permission slip.

4. The RPM group participates in *phase 1 training* – a whole-day training planned and facilitated by the RPM coordinator.

5. The RPM program is promoted to the school community through assembly announcements, a newsletter, school-based social media and any other appropriate form of communication.

6. RPMs visit classrooms to introduce themselves and talk to each class about their role.

7. RPMs plan and deliver a short presentation at Whole School Assembly that dramatizes what a Peer Mediation session may look like.

8. The RPM roster is created and RPM begins.

9. The RPM coordinator schedules *phase 2 training* – regular ongoing fortnightly meetings for RPMs to share their experiences, collectively review difficult situations, revise aspects of phase 1 training and receive additional training. Phase 2 training is the most important part of RPM training and is considered mandatory for RPMs.

The next section of this manual provides guidance on the highly important phase 2 training meetings.

6

RPM PHASE 2 TRAINING
Primary and Middle & Secondary

Phase 2 training consists of ongoing (fortnightly at least) meetings of the RPM team using a circle meeting format. Ongoing development of the RPMs' skills and understandings is as important as, if not more important than, the phase 1 training. Failing to commit to regular and ongoing phase 2 *on the job* training meetings will lead to a deterioration of the skills and principles learned in the phase 1 training.

Without phase 2 training, many RPMs tend to slip into habits of *telling* and *advice giving*, rather than using the Restorative Process and working *with* students to solve their own problems. After all, *telling* and *advice giving* will feel like a *faster solution* to the RPMs and will trick them into believing that they are getting it right, when, in actual fact, they will be coming up with solutions *for* students and not developing these skills in the students. '*What ideas do you have to fix this problem?*' will quickly turn into '*You should do this...*'

Phase 2 training meetings should take place at least fortnightly and run for a minimum of 20 minutes up to a maximum of an hour. If your colleagues become concerned about the loss of learning time for their students, it might help to look through relevant curriculum documents to identify learning outcomes that are being met by involvement in the RPM program.

Let experience be the best teacher

After time on the job, the RPMs will have questions and concerns and will want to share their stories about their RPM work. They will have encountered situations that surprised them and challenged their skill level as well as their preconceptions about being an RPM. Unless the RPMs get regular opportunities to reflect with others on these moments, they won't be able to learn anything from them and make adjustments to their practice.

Remember, we do not learn from experience...we learn from reflecting on experience.

If you reflect for a moment on your own experiences with Restorative Practices, you and your teaching colleagues will have had many questions about implementing Restorative Practices along the way. If your school handled (or is handling) this transition well, there will have been ongoing opportunities to share and discuss experiences, as everyone from support staff to senior leaders gets their heads around working restoratively with students and old paradigms and practices are challenged.

▨ *View your RPMs' needs as being the same as your colleagues'.*

As you can expect, during ongoing phase 2 training meetings you will hear from your RPMs about some successful and rewarding moments, as well as some moments that did not go so well. There is valuable feedback in this about how the information taught in the phase 1 training day was processed and applied *in the field* by your RPMs. You may even decide to make some adjustments to the phase 1 training for the next group of RPMs based on this feedback.

Phase 2 training will show you which RPMs understood the messages taught in phase 1 training, and have applied the skills successfully. You will also quickly identify RPMs who misunderstood what you intended to convey and will need urgent reteaching of the ideas and skills. Phase 2 training meetings are brilliant opportunities to teach, clarify, discuss, brainstorm and learn from one another. Sometimes, it takes practice and getting it wrong to work out how to do it right!

Phase 2 training meetings should occur at least every fortnight for the duration of their role. It is recommended that the first three or four phase 2 training meetings run a full hour as RPMs are becoming familiar with the role and using their new skills for the first time. After these initial sessions, the meetings may only last for 20–30 minutes at a time.

Suggested RPM phase 2 training activities

Phase 2 training sessions are designed to be run in a circle. Circles increase engagement, participation and equal sharing of air time between RPMs. After the phase 1 training, RPMs will be familiar with working in a circle.

Phase 2 training meetings vary in duration, depending on the number of go-arounds/activities you want to do with your RPMs and the size of the circle. The go-arounds and activities below are headed 'Every Session' and 'Optional'. We believe that the 'every session' go-arounds should be a part of every phase 2 training meeting. The 'optional' go-arounds/activities can be selected to make up the rest of the session depending on the needs of the group. We have included a rough guide to the time that each go-around will take but this of course will vary with the number of RPMs in the circle and how long each turn takes.

As mentioned above, we suggest that the first three or four meetings use all go-around topics listed below.

Every session
Start of every session: Reminder of circle rules (30 sec–1 minute)

1. One person speaks at a time

2. Right to pass

3. No put downs

Go-around: Which issues from the past two weeks need to be reported to staff? (10 minutes)

If similar conflicts are occurring in a specific part of the yard, it might signal a systemic or structural problem like an area being too small for a particular game, not enough sports equipment available, inadequate adult supervision or human traffic issues at particular access points. The RPMs often have great insight into small *structural tweaks* that can be made that will lower the number of conflicts caused by the physical environment.

Go-around: Feedback from staff (10 minutes)

Report back to RPMs from staff on management plans for particular students they need to be aware of. Issues of confidentiality need to be carefully considered and if necessary discussed with the RPMs.

Optional
Go-around topics
WHICH TYPES OF ISSUES HAVE RPMS DEALT WITH MOST FREQUENTLY? (5 MINUTES)

Are there any patterns emerging that needs to be fed back to staff?

SHARE WHAT'S WORKED WELL AND WHY? (20 MINUTES)

Sharing stories or tips that have worked and made dealing with the conflicts easier.

WHICH STUDENTS HAVE WE DEALT WITH OVER AND OVER? (10 MINUTES)

How might the RPMs support these students who are having regular troubles in the yard? Ideas such as forming friendship circles or planning and running organized games to bring greater structure to play for younger students might make a difference.

SCENARIO OF THE WEEK (20 MINUTES)

Choose a focus skill (from the phase 1 training) for the session such as *paraphrasing, reflecting feeling, questioning*, etc. Come up with a scenario that can be posed to the circle and perhaps even role played. Best approaches can then be discussed and decided on as a group.

With time, you will establish the best phase 2 training meeting *makeup* for your group of RPMs and meetings will flow well. The training demands of the group will decrease as they become more experienced as RPMs but ongoing training should never be ceased completely. Like teaching, continual learning and honing of skills is essential.

7

CONCLUSION

This manual has taken you right through what we know builds and maintains an effective Restorative Peer Mediator program. All of the ideas and trainings in this manual have been road-tested in schools and have developed as a result of trial, error and tweaking.

Restorative Practices do not come easy to schools. They challenge traditional ideas of what it means to work with young people, as well as stretching us beyond what we believe young people are capable of. In line with the restorative ideal of doing things *with* young people, rather than doing things *to* them or *for* them, peer mediation is a perfect mode for living out these principles in how we work.

Restorative Peer Mediation will act as an important cornerstone to the cultural shift that schools embark upon when moving to restorative ways of responding to conflict and strife. This program will teach an influential group of students in your school (your RPMs) what it is to work restoratively, as well as highlighting to staff the amazing outcomes that come from asking young people to have an active role in one another's school experience, particularly the experience of conflict.

We wish you all the best in the implementation of Restorative Peer Mediation in your school and encourage you to contact us if you have any questions or seek further support in making RPM hum in your school.

Bill Hansberry   bill@hansberryec.com.au

Christie-Lee Hansberry   christie@hansberryec.com.au

Appendix 1

Opposites Cards for Phase 1 Training

Salt	Pepper
Day	Night
Up	Down
Big	Small

Asleep	Awake
Hot	Cold
King	Queen
Old	New
Thin	Thick
Friendly	Unfriendly

★

Old	Young
Heavy	Light
Clockwise	Anti-clockwise
Soft	Hard
Front	Back

Appendix 2

Rules for Mediation

RPM Rules

Listen to each other

One person speaks at a time

Tell the truth

Try hard to solve the problem

RPM Script: Early Years and Primary

Introduce yourselves:

'Hi, I'm [name] and I'm an RPM. It's my job to help people sort problems out. [Name] came to me with a problem that they are worried about. They said you will be able to help us fix the problem. Will you help us? Great!'

'Who remembers the three rules for mediation?'

Be respectful, Be honest, Take turns to speak.

'Will you all follow these rules? That's great, this won't take long then.'

1. To non-reporting student(s):

'[Reporting student] tells me that there's been a problem with [explain problem briefly]. What happened?'

Paraphrase back to them what they said.

2. To reporting student(s):

'What happened from your side?' (May be same or different.)

Paraphrase.

3. To students who made a bad choice (may be all of them):

'When you [describe what they did] was that:

A good choice or a bad choice?

Or   The right thing or the wrong thing?

Or   Fair or unfair?

Or   Kind or unkind?' (only use 1 or 2 of these)

Paraphrase: 'So, you think it was...'

4. To students who were upset (may be all of them):

'How are you feeling about what's happened?'

'How do you think (name others) are feeling?'

Paraphrase.

5. To all students – beginning with the reporting student:

'What can we do to fix this problem?'

Paraphrase.

If there is anything else that needs fixing, you can add:

- *'I think you also need to [add details]'*

- *'Can you do this on your own or would you like some help?'*

6. Checking on agreement:

'So, to fix this problem you have agreed to [add details].' Ask each student, 'So, what is your part?'

'Thanks for letting me help you sort this out. Let's finish with a hi-5 or a handshake?'

Complete the RPM report and place it into the RPM folder.

Appendix 4

RPM Script: Middle & Secondary

Introduce yourselves:

'Hi, I'm [name] and I'm an RPM. It's my job to help people sort problems out. [Name] told me about a problem that they would like to sort out with you. They said they didn't want to make a big deal of it and didn't think teachers needed to be involved yet. Are you interested in solving the problem?'

'There are three rules of engagement when sorting conflicts, they are:

Be respectful, Be honest, Take turns to speak.

Can you all follow these? Okay, this won't take long then.'

1. To non-reporting student(s):

'[Reporting student] tells me that there's been a problem with [explain problem briefly]. What happened?'

Paraphrase back to them what they said.

2. To reporting student(s):

'What happened from your side?' (May be same or different.)

Paraphrase.

3. To students who made a bad choice (may be all of them)

'What were you hoping would happen when you [say what they did]?' OR 'What made you decide to do/say that?'

You may decide to go a step further and ask these closed questions to help:

Was that a good choice or a bad choice?

Or   Was that a good look or a bad look?

Or   Was that fair or unfair?

Or   Did that make the problem better or worse for you all?

Paraphrase: 'So, you think it was…'

Choose the most appropriate question; you may need to ask more than one of these questions for the student to understand what you are asking.

4. To students who were upset (may be all of them):

'How has this affected you?'

'Who else has been affected?'

'How do you think this has affected others?'

Paraphrase.

5. To all students – usually beginning with the reporting student:

'What can we do to fix this problem?' OR 'Do you want to keep the conflict going or should we try to work it out?'

Paraphrase.

6. Checking on agreement:

'So, to sort this out you have agreed to [add details].' Ask each student: 'So what is your part?'

'Is there anything anyone wants to add, or say to the other before we finish?'

'Thanks for letting me help you sort this out.'

Complete the RPM report and place it into the RPM folder.

Appendix 5

Restorative Peer Mediation Reporting Proforma

RPM REPORT

Date: _____

RPMs: 1. _____ 2. _____

Break Time (tick) ☐ Lunch 1 ☐ Lunch 2

People involved in the problem:

_____

_____

What happened?

_____

_____

How was it solved?

_____

_____

Follow-up needed? YES/NO

If yes, when?: _____

Signatures: _____

RPM REPORT

Date:_____

RPMs: 1. _____   2. _____

Break Time (tick)   ☐ Lunch 1   ☐ Lunch 2

People involved in the problem:

_____

_____

What happened?

_____

_____

How was it solved?

_____

_____

Follow-up needed? YES/NO

If yes, when?: _____

Signatures: _____

Appendix 6

Glossary of Terms Used in the RPM Program

Ball throw: A soft ball is used as a talking piece but, instead of being passed in an orderly fashion around the circle, it can be thrown from one student to another across the circle.

Change places games: These are a variety of games that move people to different places in the circle, thus mixing up students. They have the important purpose of breaking up cliques and getting students to work with those they mightn't otherwise choose to be next to in a circle.

Circle brainstorm: This is a whole circle conversation, where students either put their hand up to be chosen to contribute to the conversation or take turns to speak.

Go-around: The circle leader asks students to respond to a question and then the talking piece goes around the circle and every student has the option to respond to the question or to pass.

Mix up activities: See 'Change places games'.

Pass the smile: One person in the circle starts by looking at the person next to them (they choose which side) and then smiling at them. They have now passed the smile. The receiver of the smile then passes the smile in the same way to the person next to them. The smile travels all the way around the circle until it is returned to the person who started.

Pair share: Students are paired with a person next to them in the circle and given a task to discuss a topic (within a given timeframe). The pair may be asked to share experiences, to come to an agreement on a particular question or topic or to see if they can find common ground on an issue. Sometimes, pairs are asked to feedback what they came up with to the rest of the circle.

Silent statements: A popular form of a change place game, where the leader of the circle will say something like, *'You have ridden a horse before.'* All who have ridden a horse will indicate this by silently crossing the circle and moving into a place left by someone else who has moved.

Talking piece: This is any object that is held by the person who is speaking in a circle. Only the person holding the talking piece can speak and everyone else must listen.

Appendix 7

Links to Curricula

Australia

There are many links that can be made to the Australian curriculum, within the learning area of Health and Physical Education as well as the obvious link with the Personal and Emotional Capability within the 'General Capabilities' (ACARA n.d.). The table below identifies these links in year levels 5–10.

Year Level	Health and Physical Education Personal, Social and Community Health	General Capabilities Personal and Social Capabilities
5 and 6	• Plan and practise strategies to promote health, safety and wellbeing (ACPPS054) • Practise skills to establish and manage relationships (ACPPS055) • Examine the influence of emotional responses on behaviour and relationships (ACPPS056) • Investigate the role of preventive health in promoting and maintaining health, safety and wellbeing for individuals and their communities (ACPPS058)	**Social Awareness** • Understand relationships - identifies the differences between positive and negative relationships and ways of managing these **Social Management** • Communicate effectively –identifies and explains factors that influence effective communication in a variety of situations • Negotiate and resolve conflict – identifies causes and effects of conflict, and practises different strategies to diffuse or resolve conflict situations • Develop leadership skills – initiates or helps to organize group activities that address a common need

7 and 8	• Practise and apply strategies to seek help for themselves or others (ACPPS072) • Investigate the benefits of relationships and examine their impact on their own and others' health and wellbeing (ACPPS074) • Analyse factors that influence emotions , and develop strategies to demonstrate empathy and sensitivity (ACPPS075) • Plan and use health practices, behaviours and resources to enhance health, safety and wellbeing of their communities (ACPPS077)	**Social Awareness** • Understand relationships - identifies indicators of possible problems in relationships in a range of social and work related situations **Social Management** • Communicate effectively – analyses enablers of and barriers to effective verbal, nonverbal and digital communication • Negotiate and resolve conflict – assesses the appropriateness of various conflict resolution strategies in a range of social and work-related situations • Develop leadership skills – plans school and community projects, applying effective problem-solving and team-building strategies, and making the most of available resources to achieve goals
9 and 10	• Examine the impact of changes and transitions on relationships (ACPPS090) • Investigate how empathy and ethical decision making contribute to respectful relationships (ACPPS093) • Evaluate situations and propose appropriate emotional responses and then reflect on possible outcomes of different responses (ACPPS094) • Plan, implement and critique strategies to enhance health, safety and wellbeing of their communities (ACPPS096)	**Social Awareness** • Understand relationships –explains how relationships differ between peers, parents, teachers and other adults, and identify the skills needed to manage different types of relationships **Social Management** • Negotiate and resolve conflict – generates, applies and evaluates strategies such as active listening, mediation and negotiation to prevent and resolve interpersonal problems and conflicts • Develop leadership skills – proposes, implements and monitors strategies to address needs prioritised at local, national, regional and global levels, and communicate these widely

New Zealand

There are many links that can be made to the New Zealand curriculum, within the learning area of Health and Physical Education as well as the obvious link with the Key Competencies of 'Relating to Others' and 'Participating and Contributing' (New Zealand Ministry of Education n.d.).

The table below identifies the possible learning outcomes in Levels 3 and 4 that relate to the learning experiences within the Restorative Peer Mediation program.

Students will:	Level	Strand	Achievement Objectives
Relationships with other people			
• Identify and compare ways of establishing relationships and managing changing relationships	3	C	1
• Identify the pressures that can influence interactions with other people and demonstrate basic assertiveness strategies to manage these	3	C	3
Enhancing Relationships			
• Identify and describe the features of healthy friendships	4	C	1
• Demonstrate the skills of active listening and use these in mediation situations	4	C	3

Key Competencies
Relating to others

Relating to others is about interacting effectively with a diverse range of people in a variety of contexts. This competency includes the ability to listen actively, recognise different points of view, negotiate, and share ideas.

Students who relate well to others are open to new learning and able to take different roles in different situations. They are aware of how their words and actions affect others. They know when it is appropriate to compete and when it is appropriate to co-operate. By working effectively together, they can come up with new approaches, ideas, and ways of thinking.

Participating and contributing

This competency is about being actively involved in communities. Communities include family, whānau, and school and those based, for example, on a common interest or culture. They may be drawn together for purposes such as learning, work, celebration, or recreation. They may be local, national, or global.

This competency includes a capacity to contribute appropriately as a group member, to make connections with others, and to create opportunities for others in the group.

Students who participate and contribute in communities have a sense of belonging and the confidence to participate within new contexts. They understand the importance of balancing rights, roles, and responsibilities and of contributing to the quality and sustainability of social, cultural, physical, and economic environments.

UK

There are links that can be made to the UK curriculum, within the learning areas of the 'Citizenship Programmes of Study' and the 'Personal, Social, Health and Economic Education' program (Department for Education 2013). The table below identifies the links made within the Key Stages 3 and 4 from the Citizenship Programmes of Study that relates to the learning experiences within the Restorative Peer Mediation program.

Aim

- Develop an interest in, and commitment to, participation in volunteering as well as other forms of responsible activity, that they will take with them into adulthood.

Subject content

Key Stage 3

- The roles played by public institutions and voluntary groups in society, and the ways in which citizens work together to improve their communities, including opportunities to participate in school-based activities.

Key Stage 4

- The different ways in which a citizen can contribute to the improvement of his or her community, to include the opportunity to participate actively in community volunteering, as well as other forms of responsible activity.

Canada

There are many links that can be made to the Canadian curriculum, within the learning area of Health and Physical Education including the obvious link with the 'Living Skills Expectations' within the curriculum.

The table below identifies the possible learning outcomes within Years 7–9 from the Health and Physical Education curriculum that relates to the learning experiences within the Restorative Peer Mediation program (Ontario Ministry of Education 2010, 2015).

Living Skills – Specific Expectations

Personal Skills

1.1 Use self-awareness and self-monitoring skills to help them understand their strengths and needs, take responsibility for their actions, recognize sources of stress, and monitor their own progress, as they participate in various physical activities, develop movement competence, and acquire knowledge and skills related to healthy living.

Interpersonal Skills

1.4 Apply relationship and social skills as they participate in physical activities, develop movement competence, and acquire knowledge and skills related to healthy living to help them interact positively with others, build healthy relationships, and become effective team members.

Critical and Creative Thinking

1.5 Use a range of critical and creative thinking skills and processes to assist them in making connections, planning and setting goals, analysing and solving problems, making decisions, and evaluating their choices in connection with learning in health and physical education.

Year Level	Overall expectations
7	C3 demonstrate the ability to make connections that relate to health and well-being – how their choices and behaviours affect both themselves and others, and how factors in the world around them affect their own and others' health and well-being.
8	C2 demonstrate the ability to apply health knowledge and living skills to make reasoned decisions and take appropriate actions relating to their personal health and well-being.
9	C2.2 demonstrate an understanding of the skills and strategies needed to build healthy social relationships (e.g., peer, school, family, work) and intimate relationships C3.3 describe skills and strategies (e.g., communication, social, refusal, adaptive, and coping skills, conflict resolution strategies) that can be used to prevent or respond to situations of verbal, physical, and social bullying and sexual harassment.
10	C2.3 demonstrate the ability to analyse situations involving conflict within oneself or conflict with others (e.g., arguments, fights) and apply appropriate conflict resolution strategies.

References

Australian Curriculum Assessment and Reporting Authority (ACARA) (n.d.) *Australian Curriculum.* Available at: www.australiancurriculum.edu.au/?dnsi=1, accessed on 28 June 2016.

Burnett, N. and Thorsborne, M. (2015) *Restorative Practices and Special Needs.* London: Jessica Kingsley Publishers.

Department for Education (2013) *National Curriculum in England.* Available at: www.gov.uk/government/publications/national-curriculum-in-england-citizenship-programmes-of-study/national-curriculum-in-england-citizenship-programmes-of-study-for-key-stages-3-and-4, accessed on 10 July 2017.

Fredrickson, B. (2011) *Positivity: Ground-Breaking Research to Release Your Inner Optimist and Thrive.* Oxford: One World Publications.

Hansberry, B. (2009) *Working Restoratively in Schools: A Guidebook for Developing Safe and Connected Learning Communities.* Queenscliff, VIC: Inyahead Press.

Hansberry, B. (2016) *A Practical Introduction to Restorative Practice in Schools.* London: Jessica Kingsley Publishers.

Hansberry, B. and Langley, J. (2013) *The Grab and Go Circle Time Kit for Teaching Restorative Behaviour: 13 Sessions for Junior Primary.* Queenscliff, VIC: Inyahead Press.

Lillico, I. (2000) *The School Reforms Required to Engage Boys in Schooling 2000 ASPA Conference Report.* Available at: www.boysforward.com.au/perspectives/school-reforms/, accessed on 5 May 2017.

New Zealand Ministry of Education (n.d.) *The New Zealand Curriculum Online.* Available at: http://nzcurriculum.tki.org.nz, accessed on 17 November 2016.

Ontario Ministry of Education (2010) *The Ontario Curriculum, Grades 1–8. Health and Physical Education.* Available at: www.edu.gov.on.ca/eng/curriculum/elementary/healthcurr18.pdf, accessed on 11 July 2017.

Ontario Ministry of Education (2015) *The Ontario Curriculum, Grades 9–12. Health and Physical Education.* Available at: http://www.edu.gov.on.ca/eng/curriculum/secondary/health9to12.pdf, accessed on 11 July 2017.

Roffey, S. (2014) *Circle Solutions for Student Wellbeing,* 2nd edition. London: Sage Publications.

Skiba, R. and Peterson, R. (2003) *Peer Mediation.* Fact Sheet from the Safe and Responsive Schools Project.

Thorsborne, M. and Kelly, V. (eds) (2014) *The Psychology of Emotion in Restorative Practice.* London: Jessica Kingsley Publishers.

University of Nebraska. (2003) Available at: *Peer Mediation* http://k12engagement.unl.edu/Peer%20Mediation%20Word%2011-14-03.pdf, accessed on 26 June 2016.

Werner, E.E. (1984) 'Resilient children.' *Young Children 40,* 68–72.